Sue Waller

New Wine Press

New Wine Press
P.O. Box 17
Chichester
England

First published by New Wine Press in 1986

ISBN 0 947852 15 8

Bible references are from the New American Standard Bible

Copyright © The Lockman Foundation 1960, 1962, 1963,
1968, 1971, 1973, 1975, 1977 unless otherwise stated.

Scripture Quotations marked NIV are from the Holy Bible,
New International Version
Copyright © 1973, 1978, International Bible Society
Published by Hodder & Stoughton

Scripture Quotations marked RSV are from the
Revised Standard Version
Copyright © Churches of Christ in the United States of
America

Scripture Quotations marked GNB are from the
Good News Bible
Copyright © American Bible Society, New York

Scripture Quotations marked AV are from the Authorised
Version

Printed and bound in Great Britain by
Anchor Brendon Ltd, Tiptree, Essex

Let No Man Deceive You

Would you be able to spot a wolf in sheep's clothing?
Why were Bill and Louise so completely led astray
while sincerely desiring to serve God? Who are the
antichrists? Christians will find answers in this eye-
opening study of the Scriptures. It gives clear
guidelines for recognising today's false prophets and
avoiding the devastating consequences of deception.

Let No Man Deceive You

Contents

Acknowledgements

I am profoundly grateful and indebted to Rev Ray Borlase, Pastor of Moreton Christian Fellowship, Wirral, Merseyside, for writing the foreword to this book. His constant help, advice and encouragement throughout the writing of this manuscript has been of inestimable value.

I am also deeply grateful to Ken Burnett, Director of 'Prayer for Israel', Tom Poulson, General Secretary of 'Deo Gloria Trust', Rev Walter Riggans, Director of 'Emmanuel Study Centre', Jaffa, Israel, and Rev Erlo Stegen, Director of Kwa Sizabantu Mission, Natal, South Africa, for their invaluable help in reading and commenting on my manuscript. It has resulted in a greatly improved text.

Words are quite inadequate when it comes to thanking Robert and Daphne Beecham for allowing me to share their home throughout the two major periods of writing. I greatly appreciated their kind hospitality, their constant helpfulness and generosity in all matters pertaining to computers, and the time sacrificed in reading through my script in its important formative stages.

A special 'thank you' to Philip Baksh for so kindly allowing me the use of his word processor, especially as it was for a much longer period than we originally anticipated. I also appreciated the help of Deirdre Smyth and other kind friends who applied their expertise in English to my text.

Lastly, but by no means least, very many thanks to my editor and publisher, Ed Harding, who rescued me from the seemingly endless delays and frustrations involved in securing publication, and who, with helpfulness and efficiency, has brought my task to completion!

Many others have helped in so many different ways. Thank you all for your love, your support and your forbearance. I hope you feel that it was worthwhile! May God reward you, and may He be glorified through this text.

Foreword

There are many warnings in Scripture, not least from Jesus Himself, that false prophets, Messiahs and deceivers would come in the last days. Most Christians accept that virtually all the prophecies concerning the events leading up to the Lord's return are being fulfilled in this generation. It is therefore quite surprising that the Church takes very little note of the warnings given about false prophets. Perhaps it is because we so often see within the Church that which is false including the statements of churchmen that are a denial of Christian truth, that we do not consider very seriously the warnings of false prophets. The Church has always lived with error, what's so special about today?

I believe we are approaching a point in time when, as Scripture says, Satan knows his days are numbered. Because of this we shall see all the subtlety of the enemy, even disguising himself as an angel of light. The counterfeit will be more clever, more crafty and even more supernatural (demonic and deceptive) than ever before. It is for that reason this book has such a valuable contribution to make at this time. It draws together the many Scriptures relating to this matter, and exposes from the Word and by real life situations, that the Enemy is already at work in these days.

As a pastor of a church, yet one who is called of God to be a watchman for the nation of Britain, and Israel, I am increasingly aware of the activities of Satan blinding and deceiving the saints. I have seen it in my own fellowship, but have also seen it in other fellowships, and across the divides of denominations and nations. I have been amazed at the cunning of Satan and the naivety of Christians. If ever we needed the gift of discernment of spirits, it is now. Yet if Christians would read carefully 'Let No Man Deceive You' and reflect on the Scriptures that the author covers, while learning also from the collective experience of others, then many believers would be saved from the snare of Satan. The chapter on the 'Inward Nature' is particularly good at exposing the heart of the false prophet. Consequently, it is possible again and again to see by their fruit the bad trees.

I believe that through study of the Scriptures, personal experience and her deep concern for the Body of Christ, Sue has produced a book that will warn and protect many of God's children who are in danger of being deceived. We need no longer be like babes deceived by the craftiness of men (and women) and Satan, but can be mature enough to see the wolf coming and warn our brothers and sisters of the perils. Thanks to this book, no one need be unwarned!

Ray Borlase

Prologue
Genuine or Counterfeit?

Have you ever confidently thought, *'I would never be deceived'*? Is it only those who are unstable, or those whom we label 'drop-outs', who are deceived and led astray? Just the 'ignorant and unsuspecting'? Or could a mature, level-headed Christian who knows the Bible also be deceived?

Not long ago, the news media reported a vast network of crime involving counterfeit goods. Perfumes, foodstuffs, antibiotics, TV and radio sets, spare parts for aircraft and motorised vehicles are but a few of the items being produced as cheaply as possible and then sold as 'genuine', famous-brand products! It would take an expert to identify these as counterfeit, packaged as they are in near-perfect replicas of known, high quality goods. The unquestioning purchaser is completely deceived.

It is not such a great disaster if a bottle of perfume turns out to be of inferior quality to that stated on its wrappings, but the consequences of fitting an aircraft with sub-standard parts, or of doctors using ineffective antibiotics, could be very serious indeed. Common fraud then becomes a matter of life and death.

The counterfeit is always presented to look exactly like the genuine article. Here lies its power to deceive. Spiritual counterfeit is no exception, and not only may it require close examination to reveal its true nature, but it can also have extremely serious and damaging consequences. Confusion, discord, disruption of families, divorce, financial

11

loss, nervous and mental disturbances and even premature deaths are some of the tragic results of counterfeit ministries. Such spiritual ills as pride, domination, delusion and even rejection of the faith can also be the direct outcome of deception.

A large proportion of Christians today are involved in some form of Christian ministry. The task of leading a prayer group, or counselling and instructing a new believer, or teaching children in Sunday School is no less important than the ministry of the 'full-time' pastor or missionary. A few years ago, in the context of ministering to others, I began to realise my own need (as a committed 'charismatic' believer) for a deeper understanding of the role of 'the minister' in Christian circles today. In spite of the excellent formal Bible training I had received both in Bible College and in Missionary Training College, there came a growing conviction to further search the Scriptures on this important subject.

As I studied passages of Scripture concerning prophets and ministers, I was confronted not only with important scriptural qualifications for spiritual ministry, but also with numerous warnings in both Old and New Testaments against false ministries. I came to see that no only does Scripture set out definite qualifications for spiritual ministry, but that it also presents clear disqualifications! I was amazed when I realised the extent of biblical teaching on these issues, and their relevance for our day. True and false prophets were plainly on the scene both in Israel and in the early church. I found present-day experiences of deception so vividly explained and illustrated in the Bible, that my lack of experience and ability as an author was overshadowed by a sense of urgency to share these truths with my fellow believers in Jesus.

I hasten to add, however, that this short book is not intended to be a thorough exposition of Scripture on the subject of Spiritual Discernment! I have not tried to give a comprehensive analysis of erroneous teachings, nor to relate detailed experiences of those who have been deceived. Neither has it been my intention to expose the errors of any one sect, fellowship or church. The examples and illustrations used are far too few to be in any way comprehensive, and I hope the reader will understand that they are used solely to illustrate the points being made. Tragic stories and erroneous doctrines unfortunately abound today —I have simply made use of one or two as examples. If your situation is different, I trust that the principles being illustrated will give you the key to use in your case.

My purpose is to point the individual to *the scriptural principles* which will enable him not only to discern between true and false ministries among us today, but also to recognise the kind of circumstances that could lead him into deception. An understanding and application of these unchanging truths of Scripture will equip any Christian to recognise a 'false prophet' or a counterfeit ministry, and at the same time provide the necessary guidelines to know what to do about it.

I have used the word 'prophet' to describe the man or woman who claims the ministry of bringing the word of God to the people. He is referred to as 'prophet' or 'false prophet' irrespective of whether he is regarded as an apostle, prophet, evangelist, pastor, teacher or all five rolled into one! The word 'minister' is also used in the same way. When I specifically refer to a person exercising the gift of prophecy, it is clear from the context.

To respect the privacy of individuals mentioned, pseudonyms have been used. Scripture quotations are from the Revised Standard Version, the New American Standard Version or the New International Version of the Bible, unless otherwise indicated. Where a passage has not been quoted in full it has been for the sake of brevity, and the

13

reader will find it helpful to refer to the context and to read the whole.

It is my earnest hope and prayer that this short 'study' will help many of God's children to avoid the subtle attractions of deception and to walk in the truth. God is faithful to remind us of His way, should we err to the right hand or to the left. May our ears be 'hearing ears' when He says, **'This is the way, walk in it'** (Isaiah 30:21).

1

'False Christs and False Prophets'

**will arise
and will show signs and wonders
in order
if possible
to lead the elect astray"**

All men are curious about future events, and the disciples of Jesus were no exception. Their opportunity to question Him about His second coming and about the end of the age came as they were leaving the temple together.

Jesus had been teaching in the courtyard of the temple, and as He was leaving the disciples called His attention to its magnificent stones and buildings. King Herod had rebuilt and beautified the second temple in his desire to please the Jewish people. It was the pride and glory of every Jew. As the disciples stood there, admiring it, Jesus foretold that not one stone would be left upon another. The Romans were soon to plough it into a heap of rubble!

Looking across at their beloved temple from the Mount of Olives, away from the crowds, the disciples were eager to know more. What else would take place before their Master's return in glory? How would they know the end was approaching? **'What will be the sign of your**

15

coming and of the end of the age?', they asked (Matthew 24:3 NIV).

Were we asked if we believed we were living in the last days and close to the Lord's return, most of us would reply that the signs of the times indicate that we are. Wars, rumours of wars, famines, earthquakes and an increase in wickedness are well known signs which Jesus predicted for the end times. We see all these taking place in the world today.

Perhaps the disciples were surprised when, in reply to their question, Jesus gave them this reply, **'Watch out that no-one deceives you'**! Or as in another translation, **'Take heed that no-one leads you astray'** (Matthew 24:4)! Of all the signs that were to herald His second coming, the very first one that Jesus mentioned was the sign of deception among believers—*the sign of false prophets!*

We are all very aware of the dreadful famines and earthquakes, of the senseless wars and rumours of wars in our world today. The news media present us with heart-rending pictures of starving children, of devastated towns and villages and countless refugees. The increase in wickedness in our day is beyond dispute. Violence and terrorism are escalating uncontrollably, and the awful threat of nuclear war is a constant reminder that we are living in the last days. But are we equally aware that false prophets and false Christs (literally false anointed ones) are also on the increase? Are we aware that they are deceiving and leading many sadly astray, perhaps even among our own churches and fellowships? Or have we never really considered such a possibility?

Some of us may have identified false prophets with the leaders of other religions, such as Mohammed the prophet of Islam, Buddha or the gurus of the Eastern mystical religious movements. Others may have thought of the many so-called 'Christian' cults which are multiplying alarmingly

16

in our day. Yet, even so, most of us feel reasonably confident that we would not be deceived by any of these, believing (rightly or wrongly) that a born-again Christian would be able to discern the obvious errors of Christian Science, Mormonism or Jehovah's Witnesses, and that he would also be able to resist the subtle appeal of Transcendental Meditation or other Eastern philosophies!

Of course we cannot deny that these religious movements have deceived multitudes of people, and are among the many counterfeit religions of our day. Their leaders are certainly false Messiahs and false prophets, and the countless numbers of people who have followed them have been led far from the truth. But we must take into account that Jesus was not addressing the multitude when he gave this warning, but *His very own disciples*. He spoke to those who were closest to Him, and who had forsaken all to follow Him. He said, 'See to it that no-one leads *you* astray'.

There are some theologians who take the view that a true Christian cannot be deceived at all. They interpret the text quoted at the head of this chapter to mean that false prophets will only try to deceive the elect, but that they will not actually be able to do so. This is why many versions of the Bible translate the phrase 'if possible' as 'if it were possible', bringing quite a different shade of meaning to the plain Greek text. But if this is the case, why did Jesus take the trouble to warn us of something that could never happen?

Others say that these events will take place in another dispensation, making them virtually irrelevant to us. If it is true that false prophets will only appear in the days of a distant 'Tribulation', whether preceding or following what is known as 'the Rapture of believers', then we will have to close our eyes to the fact that many born-again children of the Lord are being deceived and led astray in these very days in which we live.

17

Today, many Christians belonging to Bible believing churches and fellowships are receiving teaching not only from their own resident minister or elders, but also from a wide variety of visiting ministers and preachers. Ministers today not only travel widely, but also often have television programmes and publish their own literature, ensuring nation-wide and often world-wide publicity. Many preachers minister with an apparent 'anointing' of power, sometimes with signs and miracles, and they usually bring a convincing message. They may tell impressive stories of 'what God has done' through their ministries, and many introduce new teachings and revelations to their unquestioning hearers. *Are they all of God?*

More than ever before, Christians are exposed to a wide variety of teachings which often have quite different emphases. Many believers are confused. Some are tossed to and fro unsure exactly what they do believe. Some are loyally following this teacher and others that one. Most believers are impressed by the 'anointing', certainly by the miraculous, and may well fear to question any ministry that comes with a demonstration of power. But do miracles or an 'anointing' necessarily authenticate a ministry? Are acts of power by themselves sufficient evidence that God is among us? Or could another power be at work other than the power of God?

While it is true that many Christians valiantly uphold the truth, often zealously arguing and disputing matters of doctrine, there are also many others who through reluctance to judge or criticise are actually failing to exercise discernment. Added to this, while it is vital that we distinguish between truth and false doctrine, it is also sadly true that many disputes over doctrinal issues have simply resulted in division among believers.

So when Jesus said, **'Watch out for false prophets'** (Matthew 7:15), He was bringing this whole issue into focus. Jesus is indicating here that *we must be able to discern the minister or prophet himself, and not just his doctrines.*

But how does one discern a false prophet? Will he have horns and a tail, and 666 written on his T-shirt? I think not! The counterfeit is always hard to detect. Forged paintings have passed the scrutiny of art experts and fetched huge sums of money before they were found to be fakes! If this is so on a natural level, then in the less tangible area of spiritual things it is unlikely that a false prophet will be easily recognised.

If we accept that the warnings of Jesus regarding false prophets do apply to our day, and that the 'elect' or true believers can be deceived or misled, then it is important that we also realise that *only those who have correctly understood the Scriptures and who are able to discern spiritually* will actually recognise and discern a false prophet in the midst of all the spiritual and religious activity that characterises our day.

'Take heed that no-one leads you astray. For many will come in my name, saying, "I am the Christ", and they will lead many astray'. . . . 'And many false prophets will arise and lead many astray' (Matthew 24:4–5, 11 RSV).

2
The Outward Appearance

**'Beware of
false prophets,
who come to you in**

SHEEP'S CLOTHING'

Sheep in Scripture always represent God's people. We know this from such well known Scriptures as, **'My sheep hear My voice'** (John 10:27), which speaks of the believer being able to hear what the Lord Jesus is saying to him, and, **'He will place the sheep at His right hand and the goats at His left'** (Matthew 25:32), which shows how God will separate His people from all others on the Day of Judgment. So what exactly is the 'sheep's clothing' that Jesus refers to in the above text?

Let us think for a moment how we usually recognise another person as a Christian. Suppose that someone

—says that he is saved,
—goes to church or some known fellowship regularly,
—behaves and dresses according to certain standards,
—reads and knows the Bible,
—can pray, testify and perhaps even preach,
—talks confidently about spiritual things,
—and is concerned for the conversion of others,

then most of us would assume that person to be our brother or sister in the Lord. All these are visible or tangible indications that a person is indeed a believer. This is our concept of a 'sheep'.

In addition to the above, what do we expect of a 'prophet' or minister of the gospel? We look also for the ability

—to expound the Scriptures and bring the word of the Lord,
—to lead a congregation in worship,
—to pray both for general needs and for individuals requiring help,
—and to show evidence of spiritual power in his ministry.

We have now built up a picture of a true Christian and an able minister! *Yet we must ask here whether it is possible for these outward signs and abilities to be counterfeited.*

If we examine one or two of the above 'identifying' marks, we will perhaps understand more clearly how this could happen. For example, there is an outward form of holiness where a person may alter his manner of dress and conform to certain standards of behaviour without it proving anything significant about the condition of his heart or his relationship with God. Similarly, fervent prayer or even eloquent and persuasive preaching from the Bible is not limited to those with a genuine experience of God. Cult leaders claim to bring 'God's word for today'—some even claim to be the only ones to interpret the Scriptures correctly! We also know that the zeal to convert others is by no means limited to those who have a true knowledge of God—it is found among followers of almost every known religious belief!

When Jesus said that false prophets would come in sheep's clothing, what did He actually mean? What kind of impression will a false prophet give to those around him?

What will he be like? In order to recognise a false prophet we need to give some consideration to his outward appearance. If, as Jesus told us, he is going to come in the guise of a sheep, it means that outwardly he will look and act like a genuine Christian, a real child of God. Even the capabilities and works of a true minister of the gospel may appear to be in evidence in his life.

Today there is a revival of the miraculous, a restoration of the gifts of the Holy Spirit, and renewal among Christians all over the world. Demonstrations of spiritual power are seen in healings, speaking in tongues, the word of prophecy, falling 'under the power' and other manifestations. Christians today are familiar with great praise gatherings and can recognise an 'anointing'. Comments like the following are often heard, 'So and so spoke in tongues for the first time, and so many people were blessed when brother Jones ministered in our fellowship!' Or, 'I saw this person get up out of a wheelchair! *That must be of God!*' But, must it?

There is no doubt that the signs and miracles which Jesus performed were a definite validation of His Messiahship. Paul also spoke of the signs of a true apostle being present in his ministry, referring to attesting miracles (2 Corinthians 12:12). We twentieth century Christians also need to experience the power of God in our midst as it was in the early church, and we do thank God for every true manifestation of His grace and power that He has been pleased to give in our day. But does this mean that 'blessing' and miracles are sufficient on their own to authenticate a ministry as being of God? Is even an apparent 'anointing' necessarily the genuine moving of the Holy Spirit? Or could these visible demonstrations of spiritual power be counterfeited?

Suppose we observe all the signs listed above in someone's life and ministry. This 'prophet' preaches an impressive message, leads his congregation in worship and prays powerfully for others—often with the evidence of 'blessing' or miracles. Is this enough to prove his authenticity? Can we now confidently assume that we are hearing from a genuine prophet of God?

Or could a false prophet do all of these things too? Is it possible that the outward appearance of both the true and the false prophet could be the same?

Could we, in fact, just be looking at 'sheep's clothing'?

Paul warned, **'Even Satan disguises himself as an angel of light. So it is not strange if his servants also disguise themselves as servants of righteousness'** (2 Corinthians 11:14–15 RSV).

3

The Inward Nature (1)

**'Since an overseer is entrusted with God's work
he must be**

BLAMELESS'

When Jesus was warning His disciples about false prophets,
He gave them this key to recognising them, **'You will
know them by their fruits'** (Matthew 7:16). He then
went on to give the well-known illustration of the good and
bad trees and the different kinds of fruit they bear. The type
of fruit a tree produces always indicates the nature of that
tree. So it follows that if we look carefully at the kind of
fruit the prophet bears in his life, we will be able to discern
his true nature.

Jesus taught them, **'Grapes are not gathered from
thorn bushes, nor figs from thistles, are they? Even
so every good tree bears good fruit, but the rotten
tree will bear rotten fruit. A good tree cannot
produce bad fruit, nor can a rotten tree produce
good fruit. So then, *you will know them by their
fruits'*** (Matthew 7:16–18, 20).

In order to know what kind of tree you are looking at, it is
not enough to examine only the leaves of that tree. For
instance, the leaves of an orange tree look very similar to
those of a lemon tree. However one tree bears sweet fruit

and the other sour! It is the fruit that is the mark of the tree. When the fruit appears, the nature of the tree will be clear for all who have eyes to see. In fact, even a blind person will know if he tastes the fruit!

Grapes and figs—the fruit of the vine and fig tree, which are symbolic of Israel or God's people—feed and refresh whoever eats them, but they are never found growing on thornbushes or thistles! Thorns and thistles only prick and hurt those who try to pluck their attractive flowers!

Consequently we should not merely observe the prophet's outward appearance, nor even his religious works or deeds, since these are all like the leaves or flowers of a fruit tree. We must also look for the real fruit of his life! *The king of fruit that we find manifested in a prophet's life will be consistent with his true nature.*

What, then, are the qualifications for spiritual ministry? What does God require of a man or woman to whom He commits the awesome task of speaking in His name? The apostle Paul's teaching on this subject gives us the insight we need.

Timothy and Titus were young ministers to whom Paul wrote, giving them clear and detailed instructions as to how to conduct themselves as ministers of the gospel. While it is true that he gave them much valid and important teaching concerning the minister's duties such as preaching and teaching (we will examine this aspect in a later chapter), Paul also taught and instructed them concerning the fruit that God requires in the minister's life and character.

Paul, as an experienced minister of the gospel himself, knew that the nature and character of a true shepherd of God's flock were of the utmost importance. In 1 Timothy 3 and Titus 1:5–9 he does not speak in theological mysteries, but declares in the clearest terms possible the standards that God requires in the life of an aspiring minister.

He *must* be:

—the husband of only one wife,
—managing his own family well,
—having obedient, believing children,
—hospitable;

—above reproach,
—disciplined, self-controlled, upright, sincere,
—just, devout, one who loves what is good,
—gentle, sensible,
—having a good reputation with outsiders.

He must *not* be:

—a recent convert,
—addicted to wine,
—a lover of money,
—quarrelsome, quick-tempered or violent.

Paul lists these as essential, not optional, requirements for those aspiring to positions of spiritual authority or leadership. Similar qualities were required in the deacons as well as the elders (bishops or overseers) of the early church. In order to qualify for the ministry of a deacon, the candidate had to 'keep hold of the deep truths of the faith with a clear conscience', and be 'tested and nothing found against him'.

Women are also mentioned, as either wives of leaders or as 'deaconesses' themselves. These were women with spiritual responsibility in the churches. Others would learn from them through their example, their word, or their work, so additional qualities had to be present in their lives. Such women *must* be worthy of respect, temperate, and trustworthy in everything; but they *must not* be malicious talkers (a serious fault in Christian women).

It is clear from these Scriptures that it is not the minister's education, nor how gifted a person he is either naturally or spiritually, but rather *the kind of life he is living* that is the important qualifying factor for ministry. Is he exercising proper authority in his home? Then he is likely to exercise his authority correctly over God's flock. Is he honest in his business dealings? Does he keep his word? Then we can suppose he will handle the Scriptures with integrity. But if he is unfaithful to his wife, a lover of alcohol or cannot control his temper, what kind of standards will he set for others to follow?

Do you think that a minister will successfully challenge the powers of darkness in another man's life, when he is yielding to the temptations of Satan in his own? He who has first dealt with the 'log' in his own eye will be the one who is qualified to take the 'specks' out of the eyes of others.

Even Jesus was tested in the wilderness. He proved that He could resist the temptations of Satan before moving out into His ministry. If we attempt to reverse this order and allow men and women to minister without their first having proved in their day to day lives that they have overcome the Tempter, how will they handle the much greater temptations and spiritual warfare of the ministry? Rather, as Paul said, **'Let these also first be tested, then let them serve . . . if they are beyond reproach'** (1 Timothy 3:10).

Reflecting on these things, some of us might be tempted to think, 'Who then can minister?' Of course, not one of us is fit for the service of God in his own natural abilities; we all fail to measure up to the required standards. None of us is a 'good tree' until he is reborn by the Spirit of God, and even then there is much for the Holy Spirit to accomplish in our lives before we bring forth the 'good fruit'—the fruit of the Spirit. Yet the gospel we proclaim declares that God is able to transform sinful man into the image and likeness of Jesus Christ. So then should not the preacher of this message bring the evidence of his own life as a testimony that what he proclaims is true? If people can see a man whom God is transforming into His own image, it will be the best sermon they ever 'hear'.

As the Good Shepherd Himself works within, recreating the inner nature to be like His own, the qualities of life and character that belong to a true shepherd of God's flock will develop. *The working of God's grace in his heart will produce the fruit that will mark him as being a genuine minister of Christ.*

The remarks of a second century Christian author in 'The Teaching of the Twelve Apostles' (the Didache) are both interesting and relevant here. He writes, 'Not every one who speaks in the Spirit is a prophet unless he has the ways of the Lord. *By their ways*, then, the false prophet and the true are to be distinguished. . . . And even if a prophet teaches the truth, *he is a false prophet if he does not practise what he preaches*'.

The one who 'practises what he preaches', and whose life bears the fruit that only a 'good tree' can produce, is seen to be the one whose message is authenticated! He then qualifies as a true prophet!

The Inward Nature (2)

**Beware of
false prophets
who come to you in sheep's clothing
but inwardly are**

RAVENOUS WOLVES'

The apostle Paul did not only teach and instruct these promising young ministers, Timothy and Titus, about the standards God required in their own lives, but he also warned them in no uncertain terms about false teachers.

In his farewell message to the elders of Ephesus he declared, **'I know that after my departure fierce wolves will come in among you, not sparing the flock; and from among your own selves will arise men speaking perverse things, to draw away the disciples after them'** (Acts 20:29–30 RSV).

Paul describes these false teachers as 'fierce wolves', reminding us of the words of Jesus where He speaks of false prophets as 'ravenous wolves'. The wolf is out to catch the sheep and devour them to satisfy his own appetite. He feeds off the sheep. They are his prey. Paul even states that some of these 'wolves' would spring from among the very elders he was addressing; that they would lead them away from the truth of the gospel that he had so diligently proclaimed.

If, as we saw earlier, a false prophet can have all the outward marks of a genuine 'sheep', and can give the impression of being a genuine prophet, what else must we look for in order to discern falsehood? How will we know if it is a wolf beneath that 'sheep's clothing', or if, behind that smiling face and those smooth words, lies a very sharp set of teeth?! Here is where we need a closer look at the prophet himself. We need to discern his real inner nature. The nature of a wolf is very different from that of a sheep!

The picture the Bible gives of false prophets is not only that they lack the genuine fruit of the Holy Spirit, but that they also produce an entirely different crop of 'fruit'! It is this 'fruit' that we will look at now.

Pride: The apostle Paul states, **'If anyone . . . does not agree with the sound words of our Lord Jesus Christ and the teaching which accords with godliness, *he is puffed up with conceit*'** (1 Timothy 6:3–4 RSV). Jude speaks of the false teachers in their midst as **'loud mouthed boasters'** (Jude 16), and Peter also describes them as speaking **'arrogant words of vanity'** (2 Peter 2:18).

Jesus came into this world as a servant. He humbled Himself, laid aside His own glory, and even accepted as His Father's will that very lowest and most despised place—the cross. In contrast, we know that Satan proudly sought the very highest place of all—he desired to be as God. As a result of such pride, Satan was condemned and fell from his high position, whereas Jesus, who had humbled Himself, was raised up from the grave and exalted to the very throne of God.

Jesus' humility pervaded everything He did. He never promoted Himself. There were times when He forbade His followers to tell anyone that He was the Messiah, and at other times He would not allow them to tell of a miracle of healing that He had performed. The word 'minister' means 'servant'; so the true minister of Christ will have the same servant-attitude as His Master. He will not feel himself too great to stoop to help with the chores at home; the needs of others will have priority over his own and he will himself help a person in need rather than merely assign someone else to the task. He will gladly see another minister praised more than himself, and will have respect for the lowliest brother in the Lord.

The proud man is quite the opposite! He speaks a lot about himself and his accomplishments, about his own experiences and victories. If God has graciously worked through his ministry, he must let everyone know! He loves to be in the limelight where others can see his expertise. He may even see visions of himself doing exploits for God! He promotes his own cause and will happily point out the faults in other men's ministries, or in other churches or other brothers and sisters. Since he is now number one, others must bow to his demands, their time and energy are considered less valuable than his. Even God Himself seems to have become his slave in answering his prayers, obeying his commands, and supplying his every wish!

The proud man is never wrong! He will seek to dominate others, dictating how they should order their lives, where they must work and perhaps even how they should dress. He will happily give his opinion on such delicate issues as whom to marry, or what to do with your money!

Whoever we are in Christian ministry, we must beg the Lord to save us from pride! Pride leads the way in all deception. Before Edom's destruction the prophet Obadiah declared, *'The pride of your heart has deceived you'* (Obadiah 3 NIV).

A Jewish sage has said, 'Greatness is the Creator's robe, and anyone entering His presence wearing it will be cast out.'

Jesus said, *'If any one would be first, he must be last of all and servant of all'* (Mark 9:35 RSV).

Love of money: Paul speaks of false teachers who are *'imagining that godliness is a means of gain'* (1 Timothy 6:5), and who are **'teaching *for base gain* what they have no right to teach'** (Titus 1:11). Peter is even more explicit when he says, *'They have their hearts trained in greed'* and *'in their greed they will exploit you with false words'* (2 Peter 2:3, 14); and Jude tells us that they **'abandon themselves for *the sake of gain* to Balaam's error . . . flattering people to gain *advantage*** (Jude 11, 16).

Covetousness was obviously a problem among some aspiring preachers of Paul's day. It may not have been obvious to the majority of the believers, but it was there, underlying their ministries, and the apostles were well able to discern it.

God does bless and prosper His servants. He blessed Abraham with **'flocks and herds, and silver and gold, and servants and maids, and camels and donkeys'** (Genesis 24:35)! When God grants wealth, it should be a blessing both to oneself and to others if used as God directs—we need not erroneously imagine that God wants everyone to be poor! Our Father in heaven is concerned about our material needs, and will not fail to provide fully for those in His service.

Nevertheless, God does not only wish to bless us financially. His desire to bless encompasses every area of our lives, and His primary concern is always for our spiritual welfare. Should financial prosperity conflict with our spiritual growth, then it is no longer a true blessing, and we would be better without it. The apostle John's desire for Gaius was, **'Beloved, I pray that in all respects you may prosper and be in good health, *just as your soul*** *prospers*' (3 John 2). If we seek financial blessing apart from the prosperity of our soul, we will give Satan a foothold in our lives whereby he will be able to deceive us and lead us away from the truth.

While not wishing to discourage the Lord's people from giving to those who need their support in Christian service, this is a day in which we need more than ever before to exercise discernment concerning where and how we give our money. While millions starve in famine-stricken countries, and while many Christian workers have chosen to serve God for far less than an average working man's income, there are Christian ministers who are getting rich by exploiting the vulnerable Christian public.

To part with your money because of an emotional appeal in a meeting, or because someone has made you feel guilty, or in the hopes that you will receive back more than you are giving away, is very unwise. The only valid motivation for giving is a pure desire to bless and help someone else in their need, and this should be preceded by prayerful consideration of the issues involved. It is not wise to give more than you feel happy about. God loves a cheerful giver, and we should be glad to give what we do and count it a privilege. There should be no reluctance, no feeling of pressure. It is worth noting that many 'big ministries' with well-known names employ professional fund-raisers to help you empty out your pockets or your bank balance!

In the Scriptures we read that God prospered Joseph in prison (Genesis 39:23)—I do not think that he became rich there! The apostle Paul joyfully reported that he had learned both how to handle abundance and also how to suffer need (Philippians 4:12). The Lord Jesus pronounced blessings on the poor and woes for the rich and well-fed (Luke 6:20–25)! We cannot simply equate God's blessing with financial prosperity, nor should we (by so doing) condemn our poorer African brethren or the persecuted Russian believers as lacking in faith.

In these days of material prosperity in the Western world, we Christians must take care that we do not unconsciously adopt the materialistic attitude of the world. We should not forget the Scripture that says, **'Be content with what you have'** (Hebrews 13:5), or that Paul himself said, **'if we have food and clothing, with these we shall be content'** (1 Timothy 6:8 RSV).

Prophets for profit are condemned together with Balaam, who went astray because he 'loved the wages of unrighteousness'! To seek after wealth and prosperity, exploiting the sheep in the process by over-emphasising certain Scriptures and neglecting others is nothing short of love of money, and is a mark of a false prophet.

'But you, man of God, flee from these things' (1 Timothy 6:11).

Immorality: Jude and Peter were not blind to the kind of people these false teachers were. **'Ungodly persons who turn the grace of God into licentiousness . . . following their own *ungodly lusts*'** (Jude 4, 19); **'creatures of instinct having *eyes full of adultery*, that never cease from sin . . . promising freedom while they themselves are slaves of corruption'** (2 Peter 2:12, 14, 19).

It may seem hard to believe that these Scriptures are referring to preachers who were actually in the midst of the early church, quite undiscerned by the majority of believers. Or perhaps harder still to think that the sins of lust would be found among those who not only claimed to believe the holy Scriptures, but who also preached from them! Yet the apostles knew it to be so, and recognised it in their very eyes, and in their hypocritical sermons.

Is adultery just a slip in a weak moment? We all know

that a Christian may fall—we are still human—and also that he may be restored again by God's grace through repentance. But unclean thoughts, hidden sin, or even flirtation may have paved the way for the actual deed. Lust may not be a popular word, but it is a common problem today, even among Christians, and alas, even among Christian ministers. In fact, in spite of the Scripture saying clearly, **'Immorality and all impurity or covetousness must not even be named among you'** (Ephesians 5:3 RSV), in many countries of the world today there are even practising homosexuals and lesbians among those claiming to be born-again, anointed *ministers* of Christ!

In these days, when permissiveness has subtly crept into the church, it may be along such lines that Satan will trap and ensnare a minister. The one who is overcome by the deceitfulness of sin, and who knowingly continues in it while maintaining his ministry, lays himself open to other lies of the devil which will lead to him becoming a false prophet.

The Scriptures are uncompromising, **'Be sure of this, that no immoral or impure man, or one who is covetous (that is an idolater), has any inheritance in the kingdom of Christ and of God'** (Ephesians 5:5 RSV).

Deceit: 'The heart is *more deceitful* than all else and is desperately sick; who can understand it? (Jeremiah 17:9).

The normal condition of the human heart is, as Jeremiah put it, 'more deceitful than all else'. The name 'Jacob' comes from the same Hebrew root as the word 'deceitful' which is used in this text. This Jacob, the supplanter and deceiver, as his name implies, had to have a divine operation for his name to be changed to Israel! No matter how clever or religious a person may be, the deceitful nature of man's heart will manifest itself unless it has been deeply and thoroughly cleansed by the blood of Jesus, and transformed by the power of the Holy Spirit.

It may not seem too serious to deceive another person by telling a small lie, or by exaggerating, or by telling only a part of the truth. However, if lying does not offend your conscience, it will become a tool that you use to promote yourself, or to get yourself out of difficulty, and truth will gradually become unimportant to you. The prophet who does not have a profound respect for truth in his daily dealings with others will not have a profound respect for spiritual truth either! Having mastered the art of deception in lesser matters, he will now deceive others with spiritual half-truths, exaggerated doctrines or satanic lies which he himself has believed.

Prophecy is an area that can be greatly misused if there is deceit in the prophet's heart. Directive prophecy is quite scriptural, though not common; men of God have at times said, 'Thus saith the Lord' while giving clear and specific directions to others. But when a prophecy is full of thoughts and ideas of the one uttering it, or motivated by his desire to manipulate and control the lives of others, then to add the awesome 'Thus saith the Lord' is utter deceit. If the one ministering feels he knows the will of God for another person, it would be much better to say openly and truthfully, 'I believe the Lord may be calling you to go to Timbuktu, will you pray about it?'

Some appear to believe that every thought they have comes from God; their deceitful hearts have convinced them that it is so. 'The Lord spoke to me' precedes and justifies almost everything they do. 'The Lord spoke to me to buy this Rolls-Royce'—how convenient! 'The Lord told me to organise things this way'—then no-one else can question it, or have any say in the matter! (Do we ever hear, 'The Lord spoke to me to apologise to you'? Or, 'The Lord told me to repent'?)

When a minister claims to hear God in every situation, the flock are often too over-awed to exercise discernment. Some have been persuaded to give their money away or even commit themselves in marriage—against their own better judgment—rather than risk being disobedient to God and have His blessing removed from their lives, as is so subtly insinuated.

Jesus told us that His sheep follow Him because they hear His voice (John 10:4), so in order to make sure that it is the Lord Jesus we are following, each one of us should seek to develop his own ability to hear the voice of God for himself. We do need to listen to others and be open to receive advice, but it is unwise to act upon the word of another when there is no 'amen' to it in one's own heart.

If we do feel able to hear the voice of God for others as well as for ourselves, then let us combine this gift with the humility that will neither violate the free will of another person, nor over-ride his own relationship with God.

The person who is deceiving others is himself deceived, certain that he and he alone is right, and is serving God more excellently than anyone else. The deceit of his own heart may lead him to believe that he is above correction, and if he repeatedly rejects the Holy Spirit's faithful work of conviction and correction in his life, he will become more and more deeply deluded, until he joins those of whom Paul wrote when he declared, **'They refused to love the truth . . . therefore God sends upon them a strong delusion'** (2 Thessalonians 2:10–11 RSV).

Hypocrisy: 'The Spirit clearly says that in later times some will abandon the faith and follow *deceiving* spirits and things taught by demons. Such teachings come through *hypocritical liars*, whose consciences have been seared as with a hot iron' (1 Timothy 4:1–2 NIV).

Hypocrisy is a manifestation of deceit. To live a lie is a natural progression from speaking a lie. The intent is to deceive. The wolf in sheep's clothing is a picture of a hypocrite. Jesus also speaks of white-washed tombs (Matthew 23:27), and Ezekiel complains of prophets who white-wash flimsy walls (Ezekiel 13:10). These are all attempts to make something rotten look good!

Hypocrisy that may have started in small ways is likely to continue in ever-increasing proportions unless at some point it is recognised and dealt with. If you dress up a naughty boy in his 'Sunday best' and tell him that he can have a bar of chocolate if he sits still in church, his behaviour may suddenly become quite 'angelic'! Any intelligent child will grasp his opportunity to earn a bar of chocolate! But if indulgent parents imagine that he has been thoroughly transformed into a 'good' boy, the child has succeeded in deceiving them.

The rewards of hypocrisy in Christian ministry are not always as obvious at first sight, but the 'bar of chocolate' may still motivate adult, or even ministerial, behaviour. The discerning believer who has a love for the truth should be alert to notice the inconsistencies which are the evidence of hypocrisy.

Some Christians have responded to calls to financial sacrifice, willing for personal hardship for the sake of the gospel, only to discover that the ones who required it of them lived extravagantly, and made sure of their own financial security. Others have been required to trust God alone to heal their sicknesses, not even taking an aspirin for a headache or making use of a 'band-aid', only to watch their leaders obtaining the best medical help when they were in need.

Religion is probably the most effective cover-up for evil that man has ever used. You can virtually get away with murder if you are seen to be a person who prays a lot, who is zealously 'winning souls for God', or who knows his Bible well enough to impress the majority of ordinary people. The Pharisees clearly impressed the people with their long prayers and seeming zeal for God, yet Jesus called them hypocrites because they laid burdens on others which they did not keep themselves.

Double standards of any kind are inconsistent with the calling of God to shepherd the flock, but they are quite consistent with the character of a hypocrite. A hypocrite is really an impostor, posing as one kind of person, but in reality another. Paul warned us, *'Impostors will proceed from bad to worse, deceiving and being deceived'* (2 Timothy 3:13).

Ungodliness: 'Certain persons have crept in unnoticed . . . *ungodly persons* who . . . deny our only Master and Lord, Jesus Christ' (Jude 4).

The word ungodliness covers a lot of ground. It is used in the Scriptures to express the opposite of upright, righteous living. Jude uses it freely when speaking of the false teachers who had **'crept in unnoticed'** in the early church. **'They feast with you without fear, *caring for themselves*** (Jude 12), he writes, alerting the believers as to whom they were having fellowship with! What a far cry from being called to care for the flock of God. A true shepherd will lay down his own life for the sheep; but the one who does the job for what he gets out of it, the 'hireling', will be too busy caring for himself!

When you read Jude's description of these men, you wonder how they could have possibly crept in unnoticed! But not everyone saw as Jude saw, and we ourselves may not see through the 'cover-up' that could be hiding some or all of the 'bad fruits' from view. Yet we should be aware that ungodliness is a mark of a false prophet, whatever form it takes, and is in essence a denial of the Lord Jesus. The discerning Christian will be able to tell the difference between the prophet who has simply not yet overcome all his faults, and the one who consistently manifests the fruits of ungodliness. A true man of God will grieve over his faults and sins more than anyone else, and take steps to correct them. But the false prophet will be blind to his sins, and will deny or excuse them should anyone have the courage to point them out.

What a contrast to the apostle Paul! He knew he could not turn the grace of God into a licence to do whatever he pleased! He said, **'I buffet my body and make it my slave,** *lest possibly after I have preached to others, I myself should be disqualified'* (1 Corinthians 9:27).

4
The Message

**'If someone comes and preaches another Jesus . . .
or if you receive a different spirit . . . or**

A DIFFERENT GOSPEL

. . . such men are false apostles'

A true apostle is, above all else, a man with a message. He is a messenger appointed by God to bring the good news of salvation through Christ to man. His message is the one, unchanging gospel of our Lord Jesus Christ.

The false apostles of New Testament times not only produced bad 'fruit' in their lives, but they had also veered away from the true message of the gospel. They were preaching subtly erroneous doctrines which undermined the true gospel of Christ.

From the above quotation of Paul, it appears that these false apostles were preaching 'Jesus', that they were ministering 'the Spirit', and that they had a 'gospel' to proclaim. But this 'gospel' was not in line with the message that Paul preached, their 'Jesus' differed from the One Paul knew, and 'the spirit' by which they ministered was not the same Holy Spirit at all.

Since it is possible for a preacher to come with 'a different gospel' even today, we need to arm ourselves with the ability to recognise it as such. So how does one recognise a 'different gospel'?

The one essential factor in discerning an erroneous 'gospel' is to really know and be familiar with the great truths of the gospel as set out in Scripture. For if we do not know the truth, how shall we discern an error? A sure knowledge of what the gospel really is will be our greatest aid in discerning 'another gospel'. Let us then look at some of the identifying marks of the gospel according to the Scriptures, and at the same time we will see how some of our modern-day 'gospels' compare with it. We will be able to test any 'gospel' we hear with the following questions:

Is it the gospel of God or of man?

Paul declared, **'*The gospel which was preached by me is not according to man*. For I neither received it from man, nor was I taught it, but I received it through a revelation of Jesus Christ'** (Galatians 1:11–12).

Paul received the message of the gospel from God Himself. He did not find it in a book, or discover it through his own religious studies. He did not learn it even from the other apostles, however reliable a source they might have been. Neither did he hear it from an angel. The Lord Jesus Christ revealed it to him. Yet he is quick to state that what he received was in full accord with the Scriptures. **'I delivered to you . . . what I also received, that Christ died for our sins according to the Scriptures, . . . and that He was raised on the third day according to the Scriptures'** (1 Corinthians 15:3–4).

In other words, *the source of his gospel was God Himself, and the Scriptures were the judge of its authenticity.* (Paul was referring to the Old Testament Scriptures.)

The Pharisees, who were the Bible teachers of those days, claimed that God had given an oral Law as well as a written Law to Moses on Mount Sinai. These were traditions and interpretations of the written Law, and were passed down orally from one generation to another. The oral teaching was regarded as authoritative as the written Scriptures. Yet Jesus often criticised the Pharisees for teaching what He called 'the precepts of men', saying that they nullified the commandments of God by these traditions (Matthew 15:9).

In our day also, it is of the greatest importance that we should be able to discern the difference between what man is teaching and what God has said. It is all too easy to be following the doctrines of man, and yet be lamentably failing to obey God.

Many Bible teachers interpret and expound the Scriptures to their 'sheep' with the kind of dogmatism that requires unquestioning acceptance. Their interpretation of Scripture is 'sound doctrine', and anything that differs with it must therefore be erroneous! But if these teachers do not also instruct believers in the principles of biblical interpretation and give them the tools with which to understand and interpret Scripture for themselves, they may well obtain a following of submissive 'sheep', but they will not help individual Christians to grow toward maturity, nor give them the environment in which to exercise discernment.

Godly teaching should never dominate the mind or will of another. If submission gives way to domination and repression it can have serious and unhappy consequences, and ceases to be truly biblical. No doubt we all agree that children (even grown-up ones) should honour and respect their parents, and wives their husbands. But must a wife believe everything that her husband believes? Should maturing children accept every doctrine of their parents? What if they are erring towards some false doctrine—must they all fall into the pit together? True submission neither requires us to relinquish our freedom of will, nor our individual responsibility, but rather it calls for a humble and teachable spirit firstly toward God, then toward those in authority, then to one another.

We should not forget that some are especially gifted to expound the Scriptures to us, or that learning to interpret the Bible correctly takes time and experience. But if we are to be able to discern between that which is merely the teaching of man and that which is the truth of God, every one of us needs to search the Scriptures for himself and be free to make his own decisions concerning his beliefs. Otherwise are we not returning to the errors of the Middle Ages when men had to accept the teachings of the Church or else . . . ?

When the great revivalist preacher, George Whitfield, was accused of being a 'Calvinist', he replied, 'I never read anything Calvin wrote, my doctrines I had from Christ and His apostles.' A true Christian has the Holy Spirit within him to guide him into all truth (John 16:13). So let us not be guided by mere doctrines of men!

When God called Jeremiah to be a prophet, He said, **'I have put My words in your mouth'** (Jeremiah 1:9). God was the source of his message and God's words were the message. However, there were false prophets in Jeremiah's day who were prophesying by another power—in this case Baal (Jeremiah 23:13). There were others who spoke visions out of their own imagination (Jeremiah 23:16), related false dreams (Jeremiah 23:25), and in their eagerness to prophesy did not wait to hear from God (Jeremiah 23:21). As God was not the source of their prophesying, *the alternative sources were either another spirit (a Satanic counterfeit), or self (their own minds).*

The gift of prophecy is a wonderful means whereby God can speak to a church or an individual through someone who is yielded to Him. This kind of personal message can be of great value, often bringing encouragement to the individual believer. Concerning this subject, Paul said, **'Do not despise prophetic utterances, but examine everything carefully'** (2 Thessalonians 5:20–21). When the gift of prophecy is exercised, we need to be able to discern its source if we are to be saved from the confusion and devastation that follows false prophecy.

Scriptures frequently quoted to encourage people to prophesy (though often out of context) are, **'You can all prophesy'** (1 Corinthians 14:31), and, **'Open your mouth wide and I will fill it'** (Psalm 81:10). But if God has not spoken, then the prophet should not speak, and to presume to give a message from God when your mind is blank, as some are taught, is to open yourself to false spirits, and so to false prophecies.

Though a man may claim to be the mouthpiece of God, Scripture does not demand blind obedience to a prophetic utterance, and those who teach this rob the believer of his God-given prerogative to 'examine everything carefully' and *judge its source*.

Then also, the prophets of Jeremiah's time ran, though God had not sent them, and prophesied, though God had not spoken to them (Jeremiah 23:21). What zeal! But is the kind of human enthusiasm we find today any different when any Tom, Dick or Harry may be encouraged to lay hands on others to pray or prophesy over them? The desire to hear a personal 'word' from the Lord leads many Christians today to submit themselves for prayer or for a word of prophecy to someone they know little or nothing about. If a prophet speaks with confidence, many will accept him unreservedly without asking how long he has been converted, the kind of life he is living, or whether or not God has commissioned him!

But mere eagerness to preach, prophesy or enter into

God's service is insufficient without the calling of God; and the source of a 'ministry' inspired by human zeal alone is unlikely to be God. Does God require 'volunteers' in His service? Apart from a meeting with God and His commissioning, 'volunteers' in the ministry may do more harm than good. They could well become false prophets.

Those whom God chooses and calls usually have a deep sense of inadequacy and dependence upon God. Jeremiah's response to the call of God was, **'Alas, Lord God! Behold I do not know how to speak'** (Jeremiah 1:6). When the prophet Isaiah met with God, he saw his own lips as unclean, and only after they were purged by fire did he respond to God's call with, **'Here am I, send me'** (Isaiah 6:8). Even the Lord Jesus Himself relied wholly upon God as the source of His ministry. He said, *'I do nothing on my own initiative,* **but I speak these things as the Father taught Me'** (John 8:28).

Is it the gospel of our Lord Jesus Christ?

'I delivered to you as of first importance what I also received, that Christ died for our sins . . . and that He was buried, and that He was raised on the third day' (1 Corinthians 15:3–4 RSV).

It is 'of first importance' to see that the Lord Jesus Christ is central in our gospel. This is *'the gospel of God . . . concerning His Son . . . the gospel of His Son'* (Romans 1:1, 3, 9).

The good news of the atoning death and life-giving resurrection of our Lord Jesus Christ brings freedom from the guilt and the dominion of sin to every one who will repent and believe. The finished work of Christ is the only ground for our forgiveness and justification in the sight of God, and faith in His blood the only pathway to a clear conscience and a daily walk in fellowship with God. Any 'gospel' which ignores or minimises these central truths is very definitely missing the mark.

Yet preaching is heard today that seems to give little place to the Lord Jesus. Sometimes it is just 'God' or 'the Spirit' who are spoken of repeatedly, or 'the Lord'. We may hear stories of the wonderful things that God is doing, or of how the Spirit is moving here and there, but often we wait in vain for any mention of the name of Jesus. Is there anything significant in this?

The prophets of Jeremiah's day—declares the Lord— **'intend to make My people forget My name by their dreams which they relate to one another'** (Jeremiah 23:27). God's name indicates His character, and the name of Jesus especially has a particular meaning. The angel of the Lord told Joseph, **'You shall call His name Jesus, for He will save His people from their sins'** (Matthew 1:21). Could some Christians be forgetting the real meaning of the gospel, that Jesus came to save and deliver us from our sins? There is not only an initial meeting with Christ at conversion, but a daily on-going experience of being saved, as we allow the Lord Jesus to have His way in every area of our lives. If this aspect of Jesus' work is absent, no matter what other religious phenomena we may experience, Jesus is no longer occupying the central place. Little wonder, then, if we also 'forget' His name!

Then sometimes today we hear a great emphasis placed upon what God can do for *us*! He can save us, heal us, guide us, prosper us, and solve all our problems. He will be there when we need Him, will answer our prayers and will take us to heaven when we die! Everything centres around—us! But no matter how wonderful such truths may seem, when Jesus Christ is central, man will be at the circumference. We will be His servants and not He ours!

At other times, in our conversations together, we like to relate accounts of Brother Smith's wonderful ministry, or of

Sister Brown's exploits for God! It seems, alas, that the Lord Jesus gets far less praise than His servants! But what has the prophet accomplished if the Lord Jesus has not worked through his ministry? And if He has worked, then let us give the praise to Him!

Paul, after years as an apostle, after receiving great revelations directly from God, after thousands of conversions, miracles and healings, still made it his aim and purpose in life *to know Christ* in ever increasing measure. Everything else he counted as loss in comparison (Philippians 3:8–10)! The Lord Jesus Christ was central in Paul's life, and consequently He was also central in the gospel he preached.

The Holy Spirit's ministry is also Christ-centred. Speaking of the work of the Spirit, Jesus Himself said, **'the Spirit of truth . . . He will bear witness to *Me*'** (John 15:26). He also said, **'He will *glorify Me*, for He will take what is Mine and declare it to you'** (John 16:14). *However, a different spirit or a different gospel will displace the Lord Jesus from His central position.*

Is it a Complete Gospel?

'I did not shrink from declaring to you *the whole purpose of God*' (Acts 20:27).

We are living in a day when, throughout widely differing church denominations or house fellowships, many are boldly proclaiming a renewed belief in a 'full gospel'. Usually this phrase indicates that the baptism and gifts of the Holy Spirit are taught and experienced, along with other associated teachings. While we thank God for every aspect of truth that is restored to the church, it sometimes seems as if other truths get lost! There can be gaps in many areas of teaching and belief, even among those who believe in a 'full gospel'!

'God is love' and 'Jesus loves you' are divine truths we love to hear proclaimed. It is, of course, vitally important to know and experience God's love in our lives, but when did your minister last use **'God is a consuming fire'** (Hebrews 12:29) as his Sunday morning text? Or, **'If we go on sinning wilfully after receiving the knowledge of the truth, there no longer remains a sacrifice for sins, but a certain, terrifying expectation of Judgment'** (Hebrews 10:26–27)?

The belief that God is holy and judges sin, even (or especially) when found in Christians, sometimes appears to be sadly lacking in groups that are experiencing renewal in other areas. But the gospel Paul preached did not leave such things out. He said plainly, **'according to my gospel, God will judge the secrets of men through Christ Jesus'** (Romans 2:16). It is undoubtedly true that a gospel which only points out our sin and unworthiness, never lifting our eyes to the Saviour who alone brings peace and salvation, will bring us into condemnation and be unable to lift us out. Yet the current belief that we must teach only that which is 'positive' and 'upbuilding' is often over-emphasised, and this kind of teaching tends to ignore large portions of Scripture carrying serious warnings or admonitions—which were written equally for our benefit—resulting in an incomplete gospel!

Some say that the cross does not imply death at all, that it was only death to Jesus, but that it is life to us. If this is so, perhaps we do not need to die daily to the self-life (1 Corinthians 15:31), or be crucified to the world (Galatians 6:14), or put to death the deeds of the flesh (Romans 8:13)? Some Christians seem not to have even heard that there is a cross that they must take up daily to be true disciples of Jesus (Luke 14:27)!

Faith is sometimes presented as if it were a commodity by which you can obtain what you want in life. 'Find a promise and claim it', we are told! But how about finding the conditions that go with the promise? Or first seeking to know the will of God? Faith that brings us into a relationship with Almighty God and requires obedience, though it is a less popular subject, actually brings a far greater reward.

In order to experience the moving of the Spirit without the hindrance of an unbelieving mind, we have been humorously advised, 'Chop off your head, and put a cabbage in its place!' But I wonder why the Creator did not just give us a cabbage in the first place? It is true that a stubborn or carnal mind is a great hindrance to our faith; but equally a vacant mind can be room for the deceiver to enter with his subtle teachings! No, let us rather allow our minds to be renewed and transformed. God is not mindless, and neither should we be! A renewed mind is as the mind of Christ; let us not despise it.

Incomplete doctrines may sound good at first hearing, having something to commend them; but every half truth or twisted truth is actually an untruth, which makes it a lie. If we do not like certain aspects of divine truth, we might just as well take a red pen and score through more than half our Bibles! Even a belief in the baptism and gifts of the Spirit is, in itself, no guarantee of a complete gospel. Nor does it ensure that the whole purpose of God is being proclaimed.

The apostle John completes our Bible with a severe warning against adding to or taking away from the revelation which God has given (Revelation 22:18–19); Moses also gave a similar warning to the children of Israel (Deuteronomy 4:2). Preachers and teachers of the Scriptures have a serious responsibility, lest by over-emphasising one truth they do away with another, thus *taking away* from the revelation of God, or lest by fanciful elaborations of their best-loved themes, they *add* to what God has said.

Is it a Powerful Gospel?

'The gospel . . . is the power of God unto salvation'
(Romans 1:16).

The real power of the gospel of Christ is that it brings to needy, sinful man a full and complete salvation. Man's sin not only mars his life and troubles his conscience, but it separates him from a life-giving relationship with God. Only the power of God can adequately undo the devastations of sin, and restore the fellowship between God and man. The gospel is that power of God.

When a person repents and believes the gospel—that Jesus died and shed His blood as an atoning sacrifice for him upon the cross—his sins are forgiven and he is declared righteous, or to be in right standing with God. He is no longer under the condemnation of the Law because he has accepted and experienced the grace of God. He has received mercy instead of judgment. When the Holy Spirit brings this about in a person's heart, that one has been born again (John 3:3). He is a new creation (2 Corinthians 5:17).

However, even the most wonderful conversion experience does not usually lead to instant holiness! When a believer begins to face up to the issues of sin in his life, he is not always helped to a clear understanding of what to do about it. The Christian who allows sin to continue in his life after his conversion may persuade himself that it does not matter, after all, no-one is perfect, and all he has to do is ask Jesus to go on forgiving him. Some preaching actually suggests this, so we should not be surprised to find many believing it. But this is an 'easy gospel', sometimes known as 'cheap grace', and it certainly does not qualify as a powerful gospel! Nor does it satisfy the true believer.

On the other hand, the new believer may feel desperately guilty and condemned, inwardly thrashing himself every time he fails his Lord. He will continually strive and make endless resolutions, but his struggle with his Adamic nature never brings him anything but a sense of failure. He will become discouraged and perhaps be tempted to give up the Christian life altogether.

If the first individual has come to belive in 'cheap grace', the second is merely trying to keep a 'legalistic gospel'. These are both powerless 'gospels'. How then does a believer walk in victory and unbroken fellowship with God following his conversion? There are many teachings today which claim to have the answer.

One current doctrine tells us that 'praise is the victory', and that if you are feeling down or depressed for any reason, start praising God and you will move into 'the victory'. Some are teaching that praise alone will bring a man into the presence of God, making any confession of sin unnecessary and irrelevant. But can you argue with your wife, shout at your children, kick the cat out of the house, and then go to a meeting where you praise your way into the presence of God? While not wishing to dispute the power of praise, it can never take the place of humbling ourselves in repentance over every unworthy thought or deed. Nor will it prevail unless we have first experienced the power of the blood to cleanse our hearts and bring us into God's courts with thanksgiving. The power of God's grace alone makes us fit to lift up holy hands in praise! Clean hands and a pure heart remain the prerequisites for ascending His holy hill (Psalm 24:4).

Some people resolve to confess only the positive truths of Scripture, believing that sooner or later they will become actual realities in their lives. While we most certainly should allow scriptural truths to renew our thinking, and there are times when we must 'stand on the promises of God', sometimes this modern 'gospel' differs little from the humanistic 'power of positive thinking' or the Christian Science doctrine of 'mind over matter'—teachings which actually lead people into unreality!

If we expect all our sicknesses to disappear by confessing 'By His stripes I am healed', or our business difficulties to vanish on repeating 'Whatsoever he doeth shall prosper', could we not then take our Bibles and confess, 'The Lord is my righteousness' while we are living in adultery or after committing a murder?

Faith is not a mind-bending process; there are principles involved. Faith depends upon a right relationship with God, and if we ignore this we will soon err. We cannot always 'claim' a Scripture without first considering the conditions, or without waiting upon God to be sure that it is His word for a particular time and situation. Sometimes there are deep roots of sin or bitterness in a person's life, which when dealt with will result in both forgiveness and healing. Or God may desire to teach us something through difficult circumstances. But how do you help a person in great pain or distress if he insists, 'I am healed', or 'all is well'? The tragic truth is that some have even died as a result of this teaching.

If we try to confess Romans 8:1, **'There is therefore now no condemnation for those who are in Christ Jesus'**, when we should be dealing with the cause of a guilty conscience, it will be no more effective than a layer of whitewash! It is unrealistic to assume that there is never any reason for a believer to feel guilty. Not only is it the work of the Holy Spirit to convict us of sin when necessary, but our conscience ought to prick us when we have done wrong! The glorious truth of Romans 8:1 is in the context of walking in the Spirit (vs 1–4). If we walk in the flesh and sin, if we become angry, proud or critical, we need to allow the Holy Spirit's work of conviction to bring us to repentance before we claim this precious truth.

In reality many Christians either bottle up their guilt or deny it altogether until all spills out in a moment of crisis or following a nervous breakdown. Sometimes this accumulated

53

guilt, when faced, appears so great that a believer may fear that he can never be forgiven.

No amount of confessing Scripture, no amount of praise, will deal with roots of sin and guilt. These require a more powerful gospel. The one who is humble enough to continue to come to the sinner's place at the foot of the cross and confess his need will continue to experience God's grace and forgiveness. A true confession with repentance will be accompanied by a continuing experience of justification, a growth in true holiness and a constantly deepening walk in fellowship with our Lord Jesus Christ. Praise, confession of Scripture and other 'victorious life' teachings will then find their place.

Paul declares that in the last days **'men will be . . . holding to a form of godliness, although** *they have denied its power*' (2 Timothy 3:5). What power is this? Not, in this case, the power of signs and miracles, wonderful though these may be, but rather the power (not just the form) of true godliness. The power to control your temper, the power to live in purity, the power to respect and honour your parents, the power to submit. The power to overcome laziness or self-indulgence, the power to humble yourself and make a needed apology. The power to be honest when selling your car, or patient when driving it! The power to be unselfish and to love others in real and practical terms. In fact, the very real power of salvation, effective in every area of our lives. *This is the power that actually does transform a sinner into the very image of Christ.*

Is it an Enduring Gospel?

'The grass withers, the flower fades, *but the word of our God stands forever*' (Isaiah 40:8). Peter quotes this verse in his first letter and adds, **'And this is the word that was preached as good news to you'** (1 Peter 1:25), clearly identifying the gospel as the enduring word of the Lord.

When we listen to some preaching today, we get the impression that God has a new gospel for our time, and that the old one is somehow obsolete! Perhaps this is one reason why so few Christians study the Scriptures for themselves, and yet they are prepared to go to meeting after meeting to hear Brother Bill or Sister Florence preach, or read scores of religious books or periodicals. Have we Christians become like the Athenians, who **'used to spend their time in nothing other than telling or hearing something new'** (Acts 17:21)?

When the Berean Jews heard new teaching from the apostle Paul, it is recorded that they **'examined the Scriptures daily, to see whether these things were so'** (Acts 17:11). In other words, the revelation Paul brought was not 'a new revelation' at all, but rather it was the eternal truth of God revealed more perfectly, and it had been mysteriously woven throughout the entire Old Testament Scriptures! Had it not been so, they would have dismissed Paul along with his new-fangled ideas!

Some teaching seems to proclaim that there is one gospel for sinners and another for saints; or that one graduates to 'higher things' at a certain stage in one's Christian life. In fact Paul does speak about going on to maturity, and the letter to the Hebrews speaks of not laying the same foundations over and over again. Indeed, we must grow up as Christians—a twenty-year-old does not need feeding on baby food! But in no sense does this mean that we are to forsake the very foundations that our faith is built upon for the sake of so-called 'higher things'. In fact many today who desire to be 'in the glory' all the time, have never even sorted out the most basic issues of their lives, or truly understood these very foundational truths of the gospel.

Before going on to these 'higher things', we should have

thoroughly understood and laid hold of the teaching of Scripture on repentance, faith, baptisms, laying on of hands, the resurrection of the dead and eternal judgment, according to Hebrews 6:1–2. How many of us have thoroughly studied the biblical teaching and established our beliefs in all these areas?

There is an ever-deepening revelation of truth for those who earnestly desire to know Christ. However, the elements of abiding and continuing in Jesus are basically the same as those through which we first came to Him. Paul said, **'As you therefore have received Christ Jesus the Lord, so walk in Him'** (Colossians 2:6).

The apostle John, in the book of Revelation, describes an angel as having *'an eternal gospel'* to preach to those who live on earth, and to every nation and tribe and tongue and people (Revelation 14:6). If God has not changed, and if man has not changed, then it is reasonable to assume that we do not need a different gospel for our day.

Paul uses strong language to conclude this subject, *'I am astonished that you are . . . turning to a different gospel, . . .* **there are some who trouble you and want to distort the gospel of Christ.** *But even if we, or an angel from heaven, should preach to you a gospel contrary to that which we have preached to you, let him be accursed'* (Galatians 1:6–8 RSV).

5

The Task and the Results (1)

'THE GOAL OF OUR INSTRUCTION

is
love from a pure heart
and a good conscience
and a sincere faith'

We look now at the task of a prophet as God's messenger, and at the reslts of his ministry. God has assigned certain duties to the prophet, and whether he is ministering in the role of a pastor, teacher, evangelist or anything else, the results arising from his ministry are dependent upon whether or not these duties are fulfilled. Consequently, if we can assess what a prophet is accomplishing in the light of this task, it can be a reliable indication of the nature of his ministry.

What are the real goals of the Christian faith? What kind of results should we expect from a genuine ministry? As we look into the Scriptures again, we will see that the ministry of a true man of God will not only fulfil the requirements that God has set, but that it will also bear the kind of fruit that will reveal its true nature.

We can safely look at Paul as our example of a true apostle. Although we think of Paul as the first great missionary and evangelist, carrying the gospel to the

Gentiles and preaching where Christ was not known, he was much more than this. The apostle Paul was also the great teacher and expositor of Scripture. It was Paul who bore the burden of the churches and who bowed his knees to the Father in earnest prayer on behalf of all whom he had brought to Christ. He was even indignant if just one believer was made to fall! The purpose of his ministry was not only to win souls, but to **'present every man complete in Christ'** (Colossians 1:28).

Paul's concern for those in his pastoral care was primarily for their spiritual welfare. Paul was not content merely to count the number of his converts, nor to relate how many were healed or spoke in tongues in his meetings. Nor was he satisfied simply to pass on his revelation of truth. Paul preached **'the truth which accords with godliness'** (Titus 1:1), and he wanted to see Christ formed in each one. What a different picture from the prophet who is preoccupied with all the glittering externals!

Paul expected to see love develop in the new believers, the kind that had no ulterior motives but came from a pure heart. He wanted each one to know how to keep a clear conscience, and to develop a faith that was sincere, without pretence or presumption. He looked for the mark of godliness in the lives of his disciples. Of any who taught otherwise, Paul declared, **'If anyone . . . does not agree with the sound words of our Lord Jesus Christ and *the teaching which accords with godliness*, he is puffed up with conceit, he knows nothing'** (1 Timothy 6:3–4 RSV).

Consequently, when he taught Timothy and Titus concerning their duties as young ministers, these same objectives were at the heart of his teaching. The goals he set for them were the very goals of his own ministry. In the 'pastoral epistles' to these two young ministers (1 & 2

Timothy and Titus), we find the main topics of Paul's instruction concerning the duties of a minister:

'Present yourself approved to God' (2 Timothy 2:15)

Paul instructed young Timothy to pay close attention to his own life, to keep a good conscience, to keep the commandment of God without stain, and to be a man of God! First and foremost, then, Paul emphasises that the all-important thing in a minister's life is *his relationship with God.* The minister's first task is to know that he has, and can maintain, the approval of God in all things. If his relationship with God is out of order, everything else will follow suit. Paul himself had realised that if he indulged the desires of his flesh it would disqualify him as a preacher (1 Corinthians 9:27).

If a relationship is to be kept in good order, there must be diligence in dealing with anything likely to disrupt or spoil it. Nowhere is this more important than in our relationship with God. The quality of a man's personal walk with God will permeate his entire ministry. This must surely be the reason why Jesus asked Peter, **'Do you love Me?'** before commissioning him with the words, **'Feed My sheep'** (John 21:17). It was the quality of Peter's love for his Master and Lord that Jesus was most concerned about. Without a lasting love-relationship with his Lord, Peter would never successfully shepherd the flock of God. Jesus was making sure that Peter had things the right way round—relationship with God first, ministry second!

'Teach what befits sound doctrine' (Titus 2:1)

Paul left Timothy at Ephesus with instructions to **'charge certain persons not to teach any different doctrine'**

(1 Timothy 1:3). He also taught Titus that an elder must hold firmly to the true message of the gospel in order to be able to **'refute those who contradict it'** (Titus 1:9). It was a matter of utmost importance to Paul that young ministers should be able not only to teach sound doctrine, but also to refute and silence those who taught and lived in a manner contradictory to the truth of the gospel.

We know that Paul warned both Timothy and Titus against disputes and arguments. They were expected to recognise and deal with false teachers rather than argue over their doctrines. Many today suggest that we should be 'tolerant' and 'forgiving' toward those who are teaching and living in error. No doubt there is a place for mercy and kindness, but would a shepherd speak lovingly to a wolf and encourage him to carry on visiting his sheep?

Jesus rebuked the Church of Thyatira with these words, **'I have this against you, that you tolerate the woman Jezebel, who calls herself a prophetess, and she teaches and leads my bond-servants astray'** (Revelation 2:20). God had already given this false prophetess time to repent, but she had rejected it. The church, however, was continuing to be tolerant.

'Set the believers an example' (1 Timothy 4:12)

No minister's duty is complete, though he be the best preacher in the world, if he is not at the same time an example to his flock. Paul continues, **'. . . an example in speech, conduct, love, faith and purity'**. The scope is wide. We cannot overestimate what a powerful sermon our lives preach. The man in the pew reads his minister's life more than he reads his Bible!

Many of us are such senseless sheep that if we see a spiritual leader acting in a certain way, we almost invariably accept that we can do likewise! If the pastor takes alcoholic drinks, then others may feel free to drink without restraint. If an elder of the church loses his temper regularly, then it can't be too bad a sin for a husband to indulge in at home or at the office. If the prophet uses questionable language, those very expressions or jokes will be repeated by many of his followers!

Some teachers suggest that a preacher who is living an immoral life, or known to be an alcoholic, or in any other satanic bond, can still be used of God in conversions, healings, baptisms of the Spirit and to preach a sound message. Of course, God can use anyone, He is sovereign, and He may well appear to be using that particular prophet. The gifts and calling of God are irrevocable. But on the other hand, whatever apparent good he accomplishes may be greatly outweighed by the effect of his example. Without doubt Satan will use his manner of life to entice others to fall into similar or even worse sin.

James taught that **'we who teach will be judged more strictly'** (James 3:1). Surely this is because of the teacher's responsibility to set the believers an example. Timothy was required to practise what he preached. A life in line with the Scriptures is essential for one who wishes to handle the Scriptures with integrity as a teacher.

Would it not be wonderful if every minister were able to say with the apostle Paul, **'Be imitators of me, as I am of Christ'** (1 Corinthians 11:1)!

The Results of the Fulfilled Task

The apostle Paul knew that righteousness was at the very heart of the gospel, and that his profoundest teaching would be to no avail if it were not worked out in the lives of the believers. To this end he taught, and to this end he instructed his young colleagues Timothy and Titus. Can we then assess the kind of results which ensued from his ministry? I think we can only speculate concerning the immeasurable results of the ministry of the apostle Paul. The preaching of the gospel and the establishing of churches throughout the known world. The writing of the major part of our New Testament Scriptures, which endure to this day. God alone knows the countless thousands of people whose lives have been restored and remade, not only through his actual ministry, but also through the inspired words of his epistles as they have been heeded throughout the following centuries.

Other men's ministries, perhaps closer to our time, have also had remarkable results. In the Middle Ages reform came throughout Christendom as a result of Martin Luther's stand for truth. In the last century, the love and power of Jesus Christ were made known, and the church born in every province of China—all largely through the ministry of another man of God, Hudson Taylor. More recently still, William Booth so fulfilled the ministry God had given to him, that the poor of many countries were lifted from sin and degradation. Slavery has been abolished, prisons reformed, street gangsters and drug addicts have been saved and given new lives, and much more—all through the ministries of faithful and devoted servants of God!

We can sometimes be deceived by results that look impressive at first sight. But after the first fireworks have died down, some apparently fruitful works leave very little to show for all the labour put into them. On the other hand, many great spiritual accomplishments have had small and insignificant beginnings, and some of God's most effective servants have been despised and opposed by their contemporaries. No, we must look beyond immediate results to know the value of any ministry.

When a prophet fulfils his God-given task, the results (although they may not always go down in history) will truly glorify God and will endure the tests of time and circumstances.

Jesus said, *'I chose you and appointed you, that you should go and bear much fruit, the kind of fruit that endures'* (John 15:16 GNB).

The Task and the Results (2)

'Many false prophets will arise and

LEAD MANY ASTRAY'

There are many examples in Scripture of prophets who failed to communicate what God was saying to the people. With our understanding of the task of the prophet and the results that spring from a God-given ministry, we can now turn our attention to ministries that fall short of divine requirements, and see what kind of results they produce.

The Results of the Unfulfilled Task

The Lord's opinion of the majority of the prophets who were contemporaries of Jeremiah was that they were not fulfilling their God-given task. He declared of them, *'If they had stood in My counsel, then they would have proclaimed My words to My people, and they would have turned them from their evil way, and from the evil of their doings'* (Jeremiah 23:22 RSV).

In describing what these ineffective prophets failed to do, this Scripture effectively outlines the prophet's task. Firstly, the prophet was expected to *stand in the counsel of*

God. The prophet who wishes to communicate God's word to men must first of all commune with God in order to hear from Him and come to know His mind. His life should be one that is firmly grounded in God's truth, showing that he himself accepts and lives within this 'counsel of God'. It would seem that these prophets neither honestly sought the will and purpose of God, nor applied the divine counsel to their own lives, and therefore were not in a position to hear and receive the word of God for others. They had not stood in the counsel of God.

Secondly, the prophet's task was *to proclaim God's words to the people.* Yet the words these prophets spoke were often contradictory to the inspired message that Jeremiah and the other true porphets of that time were proclaiming. To a people that God was warning of impending judgment because they were not walking in His ways, these prophets declared, **'Calamity will not come upon you'** (Micah 3:11–12); and instead of declaring that defeat and captivity were at hand they prophesied, **'You will have peace'** (Ezekiel 13:10). Of course it was a popular message, as messages of unconditional blessing always are. But it was not God's word.

God has something to say to His people. The prophet who substitutes his own ideas, visions, revelations, doctrines or anything else for the true word of God fails to fulfil the central requirement of his office. God declared, **'Let the prophet who has a dream tell the dream, but let him who has My word speak My word faithfully. What has straw in common with wheat?'** (Jeremiah 23:28 RSV).

Thirdly, had these prophets stood in the counsel of God, and had they brought the true word of God to the people, then they also *would have turned them from their evil way,* thus averting the coming disaster. Instead the prophets closed their eyes to the immorality, injustice and idolatry all around them; they proclaimed that God was with the people, and that He would fight for them and overcome their enemies. This message of peace and victory lulled them into a false sense of security. The result? God's people did not turn from their sin, so they were overcome by their enemies and went into captivity, suffering calamitous loss and humiliation.

Much later, when Jerusalem was in ruins and her people deported to Babylon, Jeremiah lamented, **'Your prophets have seen for you false and deceptive visions; they have not exposed your iniquity to restore your fortunes'** (Lamentations 2:14 RSV).

The work of a prophet will not change as long as God remains holy and man commits sin. To teach those entrusted to your care, or even your own children, to know God and to walk in His ways is the main purpose of any true ministry. Consequently, the prophet who is ineffective in turning God's people from sin to righteousness is not fulfilling the task that God has assigned to him.

Jeremiah told the people **'Do not listen to the words of the prophets who are prophesying to you,** *they are leading you into futility*; **they speak a vision of their own imagination, not from the mouth of the Lord'** (Jeremiah 23:16).

This cry from Jeremiah's heart needs to be heard again—in our day! There are prophets today who differ little from Jeremiah's contemporaries!

Bill and Louise were a young couple beset with problems. When they came into contact with people who said they believed in Jesus and in the Bible, their relationship was at breaking point. They were living together, though unmarried, and they desperately needed some kind of anchor for their lives. Their new friends spoke to them about Jesus and showed them how to accept Him as their Saviour. A new happiness and sense of purpose came into their lives, and their relationship began to stabilise.

These friends instructed them to read the Authorised Version of the Bible and the writings of their leader who was known among them as 'God's end-time prophet'. This prophet claimed to bring 'God's word for today'. He taught that God's only law is 'love', and that whatever anyone does in 'love' is acceptable.

Bill and Louise began to share their house with a couple who had returned from a missionary journey in the Far East. This couple related their experiences of the many souls they had won for Jesus from these heathen lands, and how God had supplied all their needs as they travelled. It was a thrilling story, and Bill and Louise eagerly anticipated being missionaries themselves one day!

It took a little time before they discovered that their missionary friends had 'won souls' by means of sexual seduction, and that as they 'witnessed' in this manner along the way, there were plenty of willing men to supply their 'provision'! They had been instructed to 'make it pay'! But by this time Bill and Louise had been taught that whatever they did 'in faith' was of God, and that an action only became sin when they did not do it 'in faith'. 'Doubt your doubts', their prophet taught. So by having 'faith' they were able to think of sexual licence as 'sharing', and even prostitution seemed a commendable sacrifice in the cause of 'winning souls'!

God brought Bill and Louise out of their deception. Their 'doubts' were in fact the workings of conscience and the instrument of their deliverance. When the truth and purity of the Lord Jesus had had time to bring them to repentance and renunciation of their false ways and beliefs, Bill commented in retrospect, 'They were leading us into sin.'

What a constrast to the ministry of a true prophet! God called Jeremiah with these words, **'See, I have set you**

67

this day over nations and over kingdoms, to pluck up and to break down, to destroy and to overthrow, to build and to plant' (Jeremiah 1:10 RSV). Why did his task involve twice as much 'negative' as 'positive' preaching?

Suppose you were planning to build a magnificent cathedral to the glory of God. However, the only suitable site for building was occupied by an ugly scrap-yard for old cars! Would you ignore the scrap-yard and build the cathedral alongside it—on the same plot of land? Would you not rather do all you could to have the place closed down, pulled down and removed? In the same way any genuine spiritual building in a person's life first requires a thorough pulling down of Satan's strongholds! Sometimes there are towers of Babel to be dismantled too, man-made structures which intend to reach to heaven, but never do. When the ground is cleared, then 'building and planting' will be successful!

If today's prophets and teachers never speak out against sin, never declare the need for righteousness, if they only preach of 'faith' or of 'love', or of victories and miracles, they neither fulfil their appointed task nor reach the real needs of the people. They are doing what all false prophets do. *They are leading God's people astray.*

The Results of the Unfulfilled Word

In the book of Deuteronomy, God declared through Moses, **'The prophet who shall speak a word presumptuously in My name which I have not commanded him to speak . . .** *if the thing does not come about or come true*, **that is the thing which the Lord has not spoken'** (Deuteronomy 18:20–22).

Here is a prophet who speaks presumptuously. Speaking in the name of the Lord, he claims divine authority for his message when in fact it has not come from God at all. However, when his word fails to come true, the people can recognise that he is a false prophet.

Even those who know little of the biblical teaching on this subject usually know that a false prophet is one whose words do not come true! However, unfulfilled prophecy is quite common today. Of all the hundreds of words spoken in the name of the Lord, there must be many which never come to pass and which are just conveniently forgotten. Yet few today would actually declare a person a false prophet on this account—it is kinder to suggest that the prophet may have been mistaken or misunderstood. But what effect will the words of a false prophet have upon the person who believes them? It is often difficult to recognise this prophet as false early enough since a certain period of time must elapse before one can say with any certainty that a prophetic word has failed to come true.

Many Christians have acted upon a prophecy or a vision given by a certain prophet, only to find out much later and through painful circumstances that the prophecy did not fulfil its promise. In some cases irreparable damage has been done by the time it was recognised as false prophecy. The minister who assumes to know the mind and will of God for another person better than that person himself, and who influences or dominates that one's decisions by a prophetic word or by any other means, must also bear responsibility for the results that ensue.

Ethel had spent her life serving God on the mission field. Sadly, soon after she retired, she developed cancer. How fortunate she felt to be surrounded by Christians so full of faith! Powerful prophecies declared that God would heal her if she would just believe. Ethel believed well enough to discard her medical insurance and to spurn the help that doctors might have given her. Yet time passed, and her hope of a last-minute miracle faded away as she suffered a prolonged and painful death.

Afterwards, some inferred that she had not had enough faith. Others said that she was healed now, in heaven. Whichever way, the prophet maintained his dignity and his ministry. But was this honest? Ethel had believed that she would be healed and live! Was she not deceived? *The prophet's word had not come to pass.*

The fellowship Henry belonged to had many attractive young girls in it, but it was Angela who caught his attention. She was tall and beautiful, intelligent and very 'spiritual'—his ideal girl. He hoped to persuade her to marry him. However, not only did they have little in common, but she did not love him.

The minister nevertheless exhorted Angela to discard her worldly ideas about love and marriage, and look for a 'man of faith'. 'Henry is a man of faith', she was told! Unity in spiritual things seemed much more important now than 'being in love', and the concept of a fruitful ministry for the Lord as a married couple appealed to Angela's 'spirituality'. Believing that her minister always 'heard from God', she paid no attention to the doubts she still felt, and ignoring her own judgment, she married him.

Difficulties ensued. The 'man of faith' she had admired in the meetings was a different man at home! Distress, tears, rebellion, hatred, violence, *divorce*! The bitterness that followed can well be imagined.

What happened to the blessing that was predicted for this marriage? Was it, as some inferred, that these two young people simply 'did not take hold of God'? *Or had they been misled by words spoken presumptuously in the name of the Lord?*

One modern 'apostle' prophesied that the world would end by 1975, and that true believers—his church only—would flee to a place of safety in 1972. When these events did not take place, the church leaders admitted that they had made a mistake, but they added, 'a few wrong predictions never hurt anybody', and 'we were utterly sincere at the time'!

Yet many members of that church had made great financial sacrifices. Some had decided against buying their own homes while others had sold theirs and had given large sums of money to the church. Others had given their savings to the church, and some had even borrowed money to help the church avoid a 'financial crisis'! Their prophets had convinced them that their money would be worthless when Christ came! Young people had decided against going to college, taking jobs instead in order to earn money for the church! Some of these people are almost penniless today, others confused or disillusioned, but the church declines any responsibility, and the 'apostle' who prophesied these events still maintains his authority.

Some Christians have received prophecies exhorting them to 'live by faith', implying that their livelihood must come directly from God. Contained in these prophecies are challenging directives to 'empty yourself', or 'lay all at God's feet', together with promises of great spiritual blessings for the obedient! In consequence some have abandoned their jobs or handed over their life's savings or a family inheritance. Should the prophesied blessings somehow fail to materialise, then the 'prophet' can suggest that 'all' has not yet been surrendered! One young woman was counselled that God would not even give her a husband unless she first handed in her 'all'!

One large church organisation teaches that God requires two (sometimes three) tenths of every church member's income as well as regular 'free-will' offerings. Many members have lived in poverty and some have even acquired debts rather than risk 'robbing God' of His tithe money, only to discover years later that the money they supposedly gave 'to God' was spent by the leading ministers on luxurious homes, private airplanes and exotic pleasure trips! Their financial sacrifices had been required to 'help meet the expenses of the ministry' or to contribute toward 'a unique opportunity to witness to world leaders'!

It is always a telling commentary on any religious organisation if the ministers get richer and the congregation poorer! Peter declared, **'In their greed they will exploit you with false words'** (2 Peter 2:3 RSV). 'False words' spoken in the name of the Lord can mislead sincere, credulous 'sheep' into a rash abandonment of personal security and thrust them into a life of unnecessary privation.

Discerning false prophecy is not always as straightforward as we might suppose. The prophet Jonah foretold the destruction of Ninevah; yet when the people repented, God spared the city for a period of time. So today, a war is predicted, but it does not come to pass. Did the believers pray it away? Food is stored in great quantities because a financial collapse is foretold, or because the last days are at hand when 'none will be able to buy or sell'. But the years carry on and the food has to be consumed or wasted. Does anyone question the prophet? Perhaps he will say that a mistake was made in interpreting the prophecy. He may even re-interpret its meaning after the predicted event has failed to take place! Then it was not really a mistake at all! It does not seem too serious, does it?

In actual fact, misinterpretation of prophecy can have very serious consequences in exactly the same way as false prophecy. Today many are acting upon the words of men who have had visions or who have given prophetic words. The vision or word may well be genuine, but what about the interpretation? If, for instance, someone has a vision of island dancers while in prayer for missions, can we then assume that this gives the minister divine authority to send brother Tom to Honolulu with a one-way ticket? Or if one hears a prophecy to 'build up the church', will the minister joyfully announce that God has now given him the 'go ahead' for his expensive new building project?

Even if a prophet has received a genuine word or vision from God, its interpretation may not always be the most obvious one. 'Building up the church' could imply that more time should be spent in prayer or in evangelism. Also, before acting upon a word or vision, God's timing and plan should still be carefully sought. God's sheep still need to hear the Shepherd's voice for themselves and know the Holy Spirit's witness in their own hearts. A prophecy or a vision can certainly help to confirm guidance that one has received from the Lord, but it is very unwise to make any major (or even minor) decisions on the leading of a vision or word of prophecy alone.

If the vision or word is not fulfilled, it will not help to say that it was misinterpreted. The result is the same whether it was a false prophecy or a false interpretation—*God's people are led astray*.

Are we able, then, to recognise a false prophet when his word does not come to pass? Or do we listen to all the reasons and excuses that explain it away? Moses said, **'The prophet has spoken it presumptuously, you need not be afraid of him'** (Deuteronomy 18:22 RSV).

The Results of Deceitful Signs

If we only acknowledge as a false prophet the one whose word does not come to pass, then we will have to admit that many fortune tellers, crystal ball gazers, mediums and the like are true prophets! Actually, they themselves usually believe this. However, Moses described a second kind of false prophet, who by his ability to foretell signs and wonders that do come to pass, subtly leads the people into following and serving other gods—into idolatry!

'If a prophet . . . gives you a sign or a wonder, and *the sign or the wonder comes to pass*, concerning which he spoke to you saying, "Let us go after other gods . . . and let us serve them", you shall not listen to the words of that prophet' (Deuteronomy 13:1–3 RSV).

The false prophet whose signs and predictions do come to pass seems to be a greater danger than the prophet whose word fails, for many will blindly follow the miraculous, especially when it is performed in the name of the Lord. Few are aware that they can be led into idolatry by these means, and may stray far away from the truth of the gospel.

Andrew was a gifted young man whose emotions could swing from great elation to utter depression, yet he was very sensitive to 'the Spirit'. Following his 'baptism in the Spirit' he began to see visions as though he were watching television. He was given considerable responsibility in the community—in spite of being young in the faith—and all stood in awe of his visions. Prophecies were spoken over him saying that God would reveal many glorious things to him and that he would have a great ministry. Some years and many visions later, however, he found himself in need of the care available in a good psychiatric hospital. He had deep emotional problems, and the doctors said that he was a danger to himself. Night and day he was tormented with thoughts of suicide.

Was Andrew helped by these 'glorious' prophecies and visions? Doubtless many of them had come to pass. Yet because Andrew himself and his spiritual leaders were satisfied with his spiritual growth—in his aptitude for visions and ability to prophesy—his attention had been deflected away from his real need. No one discerned that Andrew still needed to experience the full salvation and deliverance that Jesus Christ has accomplished for us all. If depression and suicidal tendencies remained unhealed, and personal problems were simply brushed aside, to what end were all these visions and prophecies? This emphasis on spiritual gifts gave Andrew a false sense of spiritual achievement and effectively covered up his real need.

Andrew did seek help from a Christian minister, but the short prayers and words of optimism only added to his sense of hopelessness. There seemed to be no one who would take the time to listen to his long and depressing story. Andrew's unsolved problems and his subsequent disillusionment with spiritual things led to the breakdown of his family life and caused him to drift away from the Lord.

The leaders of the fellowship to which Jim belonged took a real liking to him. He was a willing helper and did the jobs assigned to him conscientiously. They felt that they could trust him with their confidential business. When one day Jim happened to find his pastors enjoying a strong drink together (the principles of this fellowship were decidedly teetotal), he accepted a glass and kept quiet about it. It seemed that a little dishonesty did not matter—after all, 'Why should everybody know our business?' Also, a few 'white' lies would protect the name of the ministry and avoid offending a 'weaker' brother who might be made to stumble if he knew! Jim could be relied upon to relate a good cover-up story when needed, thinking that this was the 'loving' thing to do. Loyalty to his leaders earned him valued privileges, so Jim developed a 'blind eye' and learned to keep secrets.

What Jim did not realise was that he was subtly being led astray. He was learning to be deceitful—and in the name of Christ. How did he justify his actions? Had he forgotten that a Christian must walk in the light? Was it not clear that lying, dishonesty and hypocrisy belonged to the old life and not to the way of Christ? Jim was not ignorant of these things, but the 'anointing' in the meetings, the manifestation of 'the Spirit', and the signs and wonders which came to pass had led him to believe that all was well.

It is often very difficult to discern falsehood. Some Catholics believe that receiving the Holy Spirit and speaking in tongues helps them to pray to and venerate the Virgin Mary. The Mormon sect, who have many secret occult practices and believe in the plurality of gods, practise speaking with tongues and also teach their followers that miraculous supernatural experiences are a confirmation that they have found the truth! It is wise to be aware that supernatural signs can spring from 'another spirit' which is neither holy nor prepared to glorify the Lord Jesus Christ. True spiritual gifts and miraculous signs given by the Holy Spirit will honour the Lord Jesus and build up individual believers in their knowledge of Him. Counterfeit signs lead to pride and even idolatrous or immoral practices, and hinder the working of the Holy Spirit in bringing a person to the cross of Jesus where his real need will be met.

Lindy's traumatic childhood had set her on a path that became more and more disastrous as she grew older. She had known little of true parental love and discipline, and her innocence had been taken from her when she was still playing with dolls.

Resentment and fear snowballed into hatred and rebellion, and Lindy learned to escape from the harsh reality of her existence through a life of lies. By the time she had reached her early teens, her own promiscuity had led her into deep sin and perversion, and her lying had become so extreme that she felt indignant and offended when anyone questioned her creative stories. Truth and lies had merged together in the deep confusion of a very troubled young woman.

A sprained ankle caused Lindy to miss a dance one evening, and instead accept an invitation to a Christian meeting. She heard a testimony of someone whose life had been very much like her own, but who had put her past behind her and had found a meaningful new life in Christ. Knowing that this was what she really wanted, and understanding for the first time that Jesus had died for her on the cross, Lindy wept much and asked the Lord Jesus to come into her own life.

Few of Lindy's new friends could have been aware of the sad reality that, in spite of this conversion experience, her life carried on in the same vein as before. Still desperately wanting the promised, but elusive new life, she sought to be filled with the Holy Spirit. Friends prayed for her, and she experienced sensations of warmth in her body and spoke in a fluent new tongue. She was overjoyed, and the sincere friends who were with her assured her that she had received the 'baptism of the Holy Spirit'.

Some time after this experience, Lindy began to manifest spiritual gifts. She would lay hands on others for healing and often prophesied in Christian meetings. Lindy believed that she had been given a spirit of discernment as she frequently sensed what people's real problems were, and her prophecies often touched delicate issues in their lives.

Her prophecy to Peter, who was worried about his own unfaithfulness to his wife, was that God had used this experience to cause him to grow from a baby into a spiritual giant, and that God had now removed his problem so that he would never fall in the same way again. Peter's elation and feeling of spiritual restoration only lasted a few days. When his temptations recurred and his family problems grew worse, Peter bitterly blamed God for letting him down and turned away from Him. When Carol received a prophecy from Lindy that God would heal her completely from the paralysis resulting from poliomyelitis, her hopes soared in eager anticipation of the miracle. Yet not only did Carol fail to experience any improvement in her physical condition, but she also began having nightmares and other frightening supernatural experiences. There were times when people were healed after Lindy had prayed for them, but the healing would be followed by other symptoms that they had not had before, or by depression or unnatural fears and phobias.

It was strange, too, that Lindy's own problems not only persisted, but even grew worse! Here she was, a 'Spirit-filled Christian', ministering to others in the name of Christ, who yet could not cease from lying or immoral ways! Deep within, Lindy thought there was no hope for her. Her Christian experience had been bitterly disappointing and she despaired of ever finding its reality.

Lindy had married, and it was the utter shock of losing her husband to another woman that brought her to a fresh realisation of how desperately she needed help. About the same time, one or two of her Christian friends began to discern that something was wrong. One even denounced her as a false prophet—though she vigorously refuted the charge with a Scripture! Yet it was at this stage that she painfully began to break through the self-built barrier of lies and reveal the truth about her desperate need. How hard it was for her to tell the truth! How hard to humble herself when she had been giving 'the word of the Lord' to others! But when she did do so, the Lord was gracious and brought her to a minister who discerned the lying spirit within her and commanded it to leave.

Lindy's decision to seek help led her through much humbling and many spiritual battles. Freedom did not come overnight, nor without pain. But over a period of time the Lord Jesus delivered her completely from a spirit of lies, an unclean spirit, and the psychic spirit which had so cleverly counterfeited the gift of God, deceiving not only Lindy herself but also the many others who had received her prophecies and accepted her as a servant of God in their Christian fellowships.

One of the ministers helping Lindy discerned that she had never experienced a true new birth and consequently had never become a new creature in Christ. Jesus taught us that an old wineskin cannot contain new wine—it must be poured into a new wineskin (Mark 2:22). Only a truly born-again Christian can receive the *Holy* Spirit. He will only fill a clean, new vessel. Being thus unable to receive the Holy Spirit, Lindy had become a candidate for the counterfeit.

Lindy has this to say of all her religious experiences, 'I really believed that I was a servant of the Most High God—I really believed God was using me! But it was all a sham, for deep down within my life did not have any of the fruits of the Spirit. I was a tool in the hand of the Enemy, someone he used to mislead other Christians, to drag them down and bring damage to their lives. The roots of sin in my own flesh, and my pride, had given the Enemy entry to my life. But as God has caused me to know the truth in these areas, and to know the reality of the Lord Jesus taking these sins to Calvary, He has set me completely free from the deception that bound me for so long.'

Lindy no longer lives in a world of fantasy and lies. She is no longer misleading others with deceptive prophetic utterances. She is now maturing as a member of the body of Christ, and the good fruit which had been absent for so long in her life is steadily growing. When God met her in reality at her point of need, she truly did become a new creature in Christ and was able to receive the *Holy* Spirit. Her letters of repentance and apology helped to heal many of the wounds and mend the damage caused by her false gifts. Now Lindy can be a blessing to others, and is a living testimony to the abundant grace of God.

* * * * *

Before we conclude this chapter, as we soberly reflect upon

the disastrous results that follow false ministries and deceitful signs and prophecies, we may well wonder how a sincere Christian, who desires to follow and serve God, could be drawn into any of these deceptive situations. In the wake of the kind of results described in this chapter many are left stunned, wondering what went wrong, while asking themselves, 'What made me act, at times, even against my own better judgment?', or, 'How could I have been deceived when all I wanted was to follow God whole-heartedly?' From our safe perspective of 'armchair discerners' we of course are confident that *we* would never have been deceived! In actual fact deception is never immediately obvious, as those who have experienced it in any measure will hasten to inform us! So, what kind of situation might Satan use to lure a believer away from the truth?

Consider, for a moment, that you have been attending a rather sleepy church where the most exciting event of the year is the Nativity play at Christmas, or the church bazaar. Or you may simply have begun to feel dissatisfied with certain aspects of your home fellowship, or feel that you are in a spiritual 'rut', and long to go deeper in your relationship with God.

Then you discover a movement where there is enthusiasm, dedication and far-reaching vision. The leaders minister extensively around the world and proclaim their messages with great authority. Perhaps biblical prophecies suddenly make sense to you as you understand their application to world events! There may be a wonderful sense of community, and organised social activities that attract both young and old. The members live sacrificially and experience many miracles of provision. The meetings are lively and the freedom in praise brings the 'anointing' and new spiritual experiences.

You learn with excitement that God has great plans for

your future and He desires to use you. You will do great exploits for Him, and He will fulfil all the desires of your heart if only you will lay all you have at His feet. All God requires is your time, your money, your talents, your will—in fact everything. Did not Jesus say that we would have to forsake all? Your life takes on new meaning, and the promised rewards make the sacrifices seem worthwhile.

Consequently when people try to warn you about certain aspects of that organisation, you judge them as critical or as unwilling to pay the price of total commitment. Stories of confusion or tragedy wrought in the lives of previous members seem only to prove how unspiritual those people were. If you notice the leader losing his temper, you put it down to the devil attacking this servant of God. Should hypocrisy, lying, dishonesty, questionable jokes, extravagance and irresponsibility surface as time goes on, you reason, 'If God is using this person, who am I to judge? Are we not all imperfect?' Even pride seems to be permissible in a minister so greatly 'used of God'!

What a mistaken concept! Brother, sister, you have been blinded to the truth if some 'glory' in the meetings, prophetic utterance or even the coming to pass of signs or wonders causes you to shut your eyes to sin!

It was our sins—not the Roman soldiers, nor the religious leaders of Israel, nor even Judas Iscariot—that nailed Jesus to the cross! Something must be radically wrong, then, when Christian ministers, supposedly 'zealous for God', are unconcerned about the very things that nailed Jesus to the cross! Let us not be deceived! Some Christians have found higher standards of integrity and kindness in the world than in their own church leaders! Others have been led so far from the right path that they have been unable to find the way back!

Such results speak loud and clear, let us not miss their message. *False ministry results in God's people being led astray.*

6
The Antichrist (1)

'I saw another beast coming up out of the earth
and he had two horns like a lamb
and he spoke like a dragon.

He performs great signs . . .
and he deceives those who dwell on the earth.

And he causes all to be given a mark . . .
the name of the beast or the number of his name . . .
and his number is 666'

'THE FALSE PROPHET'

The False Prophet, alias 'the beast out of the earth',
described by John in Revelation, is commonly interpreted
as being the Antichrist. Paul also speaks of the coming of
the 'man of lawlessness' ('man of sin') in 2 Thessalonians 2,
again interpreted as the Antichrist. Who and what is he?

The Outward Appearance of the Antichrist

What will the Antichrist be like? How will he appear to the
people he meets? What kind of impression will he make on

all those who see and hear him? John describes the 'beast out of the earth' (not 'the beast out of the sea' which represents worldly power) as having 'two horns like a lamb'. This significant features tells us that he will have a 'lamb-like' appearance, which we may interpret as meaning that he will appear to be a child of God, a committed Christian, possibly even resembling the Lord Jesus, the Lamb of God.

At the same time we read that he will have a miraculous ministry, one that will have all the signs and miracles of a great prophet. He will seem to many like a second Elijah, a mighty end-time prophet. If the Antichrist is going to appear in the guise of a powerful prophet, we can be sure that he will be as close to the real thing as is satanically possible! John calls him **'the False Prophet'** (Revelation 19:20).

Clearly, then, as far as his outward appearance is concerned, *the Antichrist is going to come in sheep's clothing'*!

The Inward Nature of the Antichrist

'The mark of the beast' (more intriguing to Christians than science-fiction) is a mysterious sign that marks out not only the Antichrist himself, but also all those whom he has deceived into following him! Since a man's eternal destiny is identified by this mark, it is clearly important that we ask—what is it?

Our text tells us that the mark is the name of the 'beast', or the number of his name. Names in Scripture frequently describe the nature or character of the people concerned, so that it is often possible to understand a person's character by knowing the meaning of his name. We can apply this principle here. **'If anyone has insight, let him calculate the number of the beast, for it is man's number. His number is 666'** (Revelation 13:18 NIV). If 666 is the number of Antichrist's name, then it is clearly a revelation of his very nature.

Six, in Scripture, is the number of man. God created Adam on the sixth day. This lamb-like 'beast' was seen by John to be 'coming up out of the earth'. Adam was created out of the dust of the earth, in fact the name 'Adam' means 'of the earth'. Although God created Adam in His own (spiritual) image, when Adam sinned in falling to the temptation to 'be like God', he in fact lost his real likeness to God (through spiritual death), and his earthly nature became vulnerable to the control of Satan. Man's nature is subsequently described as 'fallen'.

The Antichrist, then, embodies this fallen nature of Adam. His most significant characteristic is pride. **'The man of lawlessness . . . opposes and exalts himself above every so-called god or object of worship, so that he takes his seat in the temple of God, displaying himself as being God'** (2 Thessalonians 2:3–4). The same pride that arose in Satan when he attempted to set himself up in the place of (and therefore in opposition to) God, now rises up in this man of earth, the Antichrist, and sums up all the pride of fallen man in this one unqualified act of rebellion.

Paul names the Antichrist as the 'man of lawlessness' or 'man of sin'. Even though he performs great miracles, signs and wonders, and though he even puts himself in the place of God, his very name implies that his nature is *sinful* and *lawless*.

Without question then, even in spite of his very deceptive 'sheep's clothing', *the Antichrist's nature is that of a 'wolf' rather than a 'sheep'!*

In contrast, the name of Jesus and the name of the Father mark the foreheads of the 'redeemed of the Lamb'. The mark of God is upon them. **'Behold, the Lamb was standing on Mount Zion, and with Him one hundred** and forty four thousand, having His name and the name of His Father written on their foreheads' (Revelation 14:1).

God knows the mark with which each one of us is marked, and He is well able to identify His true children. He knows whether we are showing forth the nature of Christ or the fallen nature of Adam. Whether in fact we manifest the fruit of the Spirit or the works of the flesh. Jesus gave us a similar picture when He spoke of separating the sheep and the goats on the Day of Judgment. The difference is not only that they have behaved differently, but also that their fundamental natures are different.

Even though a person may claim to know God on the basis of having experienced the miraculous, unless this experience is accompanied by a change of heart and by the transformation of his very nature through the Holy Spirit's work of regeneration, he will not be counted among 'the redeemed of the Lamb'. The redeemed have the nature of the Lamb. *They are marked with His name!*

The Antichrist, however, manifests the nature of man in his sinful, unregenerate state, unchanged and unredeemed! This is 'the number of his name'. It is 666. Man, all man, and nothing but man! *This is 'the mark of the beast'.*

The Work of the Antichrist

What will be the purpose of the Antichrist's coming? What work will he accomplish here on earth? The 'beast' who had horns like a lamb, and who came up out of the earth, also 'spoke as a dragon'. In other words, he is the mouthpiece of Satan, and although he may have much to say that will sound good and even true, yet the source of his message is Satan himself, the Deceiver. The Antichrist will perform his miraculous signs through the power of Satan, but they will appear as God-given miracles. These signs and miraculous acts which he is able to perform will so impress and dazzle the people, that they will be blinded to his deceptive words and be easily led astray. His words and his works will unite to *'deceive those who dwell on the earth'*.

Gifts and miracles that operate through unregenerate human nature are counterfeit and deceptive, and will lead men away from God rather than to Him. Such gifts actually blind a person to his need of salvation and righteousness, and close his ears to the true word of God. The power of God is intended for cleansed and purified vessels. God will not choose to fill a vessel with His power if it has neither been cleansed by the blood of Jesus, nor is being sanctified by the ongoing work of the Holy Spirit. Satan will choose such a vessel for his counterfeit gifts. The miraculous together with sin is antichrist.

The work of the Antichrist is to lead multitudes away from God. They will end up bowing to Satan, utterly deceived, having the same mark as the Antichrist himself, 666. In other words, in spite of all the miracles they may have experienced, their sinful nature remains sinful, the power of Jesus is not at work to change that Adamic nature. They are not saved. They are not redeemed. *They are deceived.*

'The man of lawlessness . . . whose coming is in accord with the activity of Satan, with all power and signs and false wonders, and with all the deception of wickedness for those who perish, because they did not receive the love of the truth so as to be saved' (2 Thessalonians 2:3, 9–10).

The Antichrist (2)

'Beloved do not believe every spirit,
but test the spirits
to see whether they are of God, for

MANY FALSE PROPHETS

have gone out into the world'

Who are the antichrists? The apostle John tells us that
many false prophets, many deceivers, many antichrists have
arisen. He declares that the spirit of antichrist is already in
the world. **'Just as you heard that Antichrist is
coming, even now many antichrists have arisen;
from this we know that it is the last hour'** (1 John
2:18). If many antichrists had already arisen in the early
church, signifying that it was 'the last hour', what about our
day and the hour in which we are now living?

In warning the believers, John does not differentiate
between false prophets, deceivers or antichrists. He speaks
of antichrists as **'trying to deceive you'** (1 John 2:26), of
false prophets as having **'the spirit of antichrist'** (1 John
4:1–3), and of deceivers he writes, **'this is the deceiver
and the antichrist'** (2 John 7). So when John tells us to
'test the spirits', the reason he gives is **'because many**

false prophets have gone out into the world'. He is, in fact, exhorting us to exercise our discernment when hearing the prophet's message, to see whether he ministers by the Spirit of God or by the spirit of antichrist!

How, then, do we discern the spirit of antichrist from the Spirit of God in a prophet? At first sight, looking at the following Scriptures, it would appear to be rather obvious and perhaps relatively easy to discern.

> **'By this you know the Spirit of God: every spirit which confesses that Jesus Christ has come in the flesh is of God, and every spirit which does not confess Jesus is not of God. This is the spirit of antichrist, of which you heard that it was coming, and now it is in the world already'** (1 John 4:2–3 RSV).
>
> **'For many deceivers have gone out into the world, those who do not acknowledge Jesus Christ as coming in the flesh. This is the deceiver and the antichrist'** (2 John 7).
>
> **'Who is the liar but he who denies that Jesus is the Christ? This is the antichrist, the one who denies the Father and the Son'** (1 John 2:22 RSV).

The spirit of antichrist, it appears, simply denies Jesus, refusing to acknowledge Him as the Messiah (the Christ), or as coming in the flesh, whereas the Spirit of God confesses Jesus and acknowledges that he has come in the flesh. So we would expect an outright denial of Jesus, in one way or another, by the one who has the spirit of antichrist.

If this is the case, it would be very easy to pass over these verses, thinking that they neither apply to ourselves nor to anyone else we know. Most Christian preachers, and even many who belong to sects or cults, at least profess to believe that Jesus came to earth in human form and is the Messiah.

Of those who do not, we feel confident that we would recognise their unscriptural stand. But there is also a truth hidden here that needs to be spiritually discerned. What does it mean to confess or deny Jesus? Is it only verbal acknowledgment that is indicated?

We have already mentioned that there are Christians today who speak mainly of 'the Spirit' and 'God', even to the point of rarely proclaiming Jesus at all. Some rarely preach about Jesus and the work He came to do, preferring more 'up-to-date' doctrines. These preachers might not deny Jesus outright, yet there is a subtle denying of Him in both doctrine and practice.

On the other hand, some Christian groups speak almost exclusively about Jesus, and rarely mention the Father or the Holy Spirit! Can we assume, therefore, that they are free from the spirit of antichrist?

Among those who confess their sound beliefs regarding the person of Jesus, are many who also claim that He has come in their own 'flesh' (their hearts), and that he is their personal Messiah. Yet among even these there can be some whose lives deny its reality. Outwardly they may confess Jesus, but at home and at work there is no evidence of the life and nature of Jesus to be seen—only the works of their own flesh (Galatians 5:19–21).

Paul says of certain false teachers, **'They profess to know God,** *but by their deeds they deny Him'* (Titus 1:16). It is possible to deny Jesus verbally, like Peter did (although he quickly repented), but it is also possible to deny Him by our deeds while still professing to know Him! If the way we live contradicts the truth that Jesus came to save us from sin and recreate us in His image, then we are as surely denying Him as if we were saying so verbally.

A young believer who has not yet learned to **'put to death the deeds of the flesh'** (see Romans 8:13 and Colossians 3:5) may yet show his true nature by the grief he feels over the sin in his life, and a repentant attitude will still mark him as a true believer. But one who has no desire to change his ways, but knowingly continues to practise deeds which deny the Lord Jesus Christ while he still professes and proclaims Him—this one has the spirit of antichrist.

Confessing Jesus is much more than a mere verbal acknowledgment of certain truths. Paul declared that Timothy had made 'the good confession' by publicly testifying to his faith in Christ. He likens it to the confession of faith that Jesus Himself made when standing before Pontius Pilate (1 Timothy 6:12–14). Jesus gave testimony to the truth when compromise might have saved His life. So also did many of the early Christians. In fact our word 'martyr' is derived from the Greek word for witness, 'martus', and Jesus is called *the faithful and true Witness* (Revelation 3:14). It may be in the hour of testing (though not necessarily in literal death) that we prove by both our words and our actions whether we truly confess Jesus or deny Him.

Jesus spoke of the Pharisees in the words of Isaiah, **'This people honours me with their lips, but their heart is far away from Me'** (Matthew 15:8). The Pharisees were very vocal in their profession of God, yet they had 'explained' the Scriptures in such a way that at times they became a means to avoid certain commandments rather than keep them. This was in essence a denial of God.

It has been said that in the last days, in 'the falling away', Christians will be teaching in Christ's name the exact opposite of what Jesus Himself actually taught. They will misuse the Scriptures to support their deceptive teachings and to justify their selfish and ungodly lives. In this way they will eventually deny everything Christ came to do and teach. These are unequivocally *anti* Christ!

Just as the Pharisees sought to avoid the spirit and real

meaning of the Law at times by a legalistic adherence to the letter of it (which is why Jesus called them hypocrites), we Christians are also capable of the same deceptive tactics. Have none of us ever prided ourselves that we 'did not tell a lie' while inwardly trying to quieten the guilt that followed an act of deliberate deceit?

Teaching that permits a disregard for the real meaning of the words and commands of the Lord Jesus Christ springs from the spirit of antichrist. This is dangerous ground. In our day, certainly in many of the new movements, sects and cults, and perhaps even in some of our own churches and fellowships, this is already happening. We must be alert. The spirit of anti-Christ is in our midst!

False prophets, false teachers, false apostles and deceivers, all are tools in the hand of Satan, the one who opposes God. They operate by the spirit of antichrist. In fact *they are the antichrists*. They will subtly deny Jesus, and will be used by Satan to pave the way for the coming of *the Antichrist* by conditioning multitudes blindly to follow the miraculous while being careless concerning sin and falsehood.

Do you feel confident that you will recognise the Antichrist when he appears? Perhaps the belief that all Christians are to be 'raptured' before the Antichrist comes leads you to assume that this does not really concern you? Do not be deceived! Ask yourself rather, 'Can I discern the spirit of antichrist, and can I recognise *the antichrists* that are in our very midst *NOW*?'

7

The Reasons and the Remedy

**'Test yourselves
to see if you are in the faith**

EXAMINE YOURSELVES!'

Why should a 'born-again' Christian be vulnerable to deception? Are there any valid reasons why some are deceived and not others? If we do discover areas of vulnerability in our lives, can these be remedied so that we can safely avoid the pitfalls of deception?

Whether we think we have ever been deceived or not, each one of us would do well to ask himself this question, 'Is there any possible ground *within me* where the seeds of deception could be sown?' If we can discover a *reason* for being deceived, we will have taken the first step toward finding the *remedy*! So then, let us at this point *'examine ourselves'*, and see if we can find any vulnerable areas of our lives that might give an opportunity to the Deceiver.

A Shallow Experience of Conversion

Man has been going astray since the fall of Adam; he needs to turn around and change direction in order to walk in fellowship with God. We call this event in our lives 'conversion'. No doubt we agree about the necessity of conversion, but just what is it?

People come to the Lord in many ways, and the following examples are only briefly mentioned here in order to illustrate a point. There is not space to go into everyone's conversion experience.

Some evangelists say that it is as simple as the ABC; a) admit that you are a sinner; b) believe that Jesus Christ died for you; and c) come to Him. If you take these three steps in sincerity, you will become a Christian. You will be converted. Other preachers, after proclaiming a message about Christ, will encourage the people to repeat a 'sinner's prayer', saying that in order to be converted 'all you have to do is accept Jesus into your heart'. In other circles enquirers are prayed for with the laying on of hands; some speak in tongues, others may even 'fall out', but whatever manifestation ensues it is taken as evidence that the person has met with God and is therefore converted.

While it is certainly true that many are brought into a genuine relationship with the Lord in spite of very little knowledge of what it is all about, there are also many supposed conversions that are not genuine at all, while so many others are unquestionably shallow.

What do the Scriptures tell us about conversion? Before commissioning His disciples, Jesus told them **'that repentance for forgiveness of sins should be proclaimed in His name to all the nations'** (Luke 24:47). So when Peter preached in Jerusalem to the Jews, he said, **'Repent then, and turn to God, so that your sins may be wiped out'** (Acts 3:19). Paul also, at Athens, declared to the Gentiles, **'God commands all men everywhere to repent'** (Acts 17:30).

Repentance is the essence of conversion. True and deep repentance prepares the heart to receive the word of God, and is the prerequisite of genuine faith. If this is so, then

93

why do so many sincere people fail to experience any depth of repentance at their conversion?

When the true gospel message is proclaimed in the power of the Holy Spirit, it exposes man's sinfulness in the light of the holiness of God. Conviction of sin is essential to bring a person to repentance. The Scripture says, **'He who conceals his transgressions will not prosper, but he who confesses and forsakes them will obtain mercy'** (Proverbs 28:13 RSV). There is more to obtaining God's mercy than just admitting that you are a sinner, or even receiving Jesus into your heart. All sin, (not just that which is socially unacceptable) needs to be confessed and forsaken. A true turning from sin can then be accompanied by a wholehearted turning to God, which together constitute a genuine conversion.

Today we seldom hear teaching on the important part that confession of sin and restitution play in conversion. But if someone stole your car, then afterwards claimed to be converted, would it suffice that he had asked God's forgiveness? Would you not expect him to confess the theft to you and return your car? In fact, if he did not, I think you would doubt the genuineness of his conversion! Yet in less obvious ways, often many wrongs are swept under the carpet at conversion instead of being cleared up and put right. Restitution is clearly taught in the Scriptures (Exodus 22); and Jesus Himself did not discourage Zacchaeus from practising it at his conversion. In fact it was only after Zacchaeus had declared his intent to make restitution to those he had cheated that Jesus declared him converted, saying, **'Today salvation has come to this house'** (Luke 19:9).

Consequently, if you have never thoroughly separated from sinful ways, or, as far as possible, made past wrongs right, it would appear that your experience of conversion did not go very deep—even if you did accept Jesus into your heart. *Accepting Christ is unquestionably important, but if it is the beginning and end of your repentance, it will result in a shallow conversion, leaving you vulnerable to deception.*

Continuance in Sin

One of the great doctrines of the New Testament is called 'justification by faith'. Sinful man is pardoned and accounted righteous before God through faith in the atoning death of our Lord Jesus Christ.

The great reformer Martin Luther brought this truth to light in the midst of medieval darkness, when men were being taught they must purchase divine pardon with silver or gold! To emphasise that it is through faith that man is justified, rather than by works, he translated Romans 5:1 thus: 'Having been justified by faith alone, we have peace with God'. The word 'alone' is not actually in the original text. While we can *only* be justified by faith, and not by works, genuine faith is never *alone*; it is always accompanied by corresponding deeds and actions and by a quality of life that proves its reality. In fact, Luther himself said, 'though we are saved by faith alone, *faith cannot remain alone*'.

The apostle James tells us, 'faith without works is dead', otherwise, as he points out, even the devils can say that they believe! If a devil can be a 'believer', something must be wrong somewhere!

Through faith in Christ, we are able to sing the chorus which says, 'When God looks at me, He sees not what I used to be, but He sees Jesus'. When God has forgiven our past sins, He does not remember them against us ever again. The blood of Jesus has blotted them out. But can we therefore assume that God closes His eyes to every wrong thing we do subsequently, and that we can sing, in effect, 'When God looks at me, He sees not what I've said and done today, but He sees Jesus'? If we assume it to be so, we have come dangerously near to the falsehood Paul had to correct when he asked, **'Shall we go on sinning so that grace might increase?'** (Romans 6:1).

The very same apostle who brought us the doctrine of justification by faith answers his own question like this, 'May it never be! How shall we who died to sin still live in it?' The truth is, that not only has Jesus died, but we, in fact, have died to sin too—that is, if our faith is genuine! This is the whole point of what Paul is teaching. There is no cover-up here for any continuance in sin.

A shallow conversion is likely to be followed by a constant struggle and failure in the battle against sin. Sooner or later, either one faces up to reality and allows God to deal with the deep-down things, or else one's interpretation of 'justification' carries one over the line into deception. When we start to think that all is well in spite of sin remaining in our lives, we open a door wide to the Deceiver to enter with all kinds of other lies.

A willingness to bow in repentance over sin, however small it may seem, prepares the heart to receive an ever-increasing experience of salvation—a progressive deliverance from sin that leads to growth in true holiness.

A man whom God has used in one of the greatest revivals of our day has said, 'The smallest sin is more deadly than the worst kind of cancer'! The Christian who does not take sin seriously, nor deal with it ruthlessly by the means God has provided, not only despises the grace of God, but also lays himself open to deception.

Carnality

'Are you not of the flesh, and behaving like ordinary men?' Paul asks the Corinthians (1 Corinthians 3:3). One would have thought that these Christians were very spiritual—doubtless they thought so themselves, as they certainly had an abundance of spiritual gifts operating in their meetings! But there was jealousy, there were divisions in the church, there was serious sin among them. They exalted and followed man—Peter, Paul and Apollos had ministered there! There was pride and boasting. There were even individuals who said, **'I am of Christ'** (1 Corinthians 1:12)—these felt confident that they were the most spiritual of all! Yet Paul calls them all unspiritual, fleshly, carnal. Who knows along what lines they might not have erred had Paul not written two long corrective letters to them?

The natural man seeks his own fulfilment. His desire to be somebody or to do something of value can carry over into a religious form. Prophecies that promise great things for a person can be very attractive to a frustrated Christian—they actually appeal to the natural man, to his carnality, but because of the religious nature of the prophecies, they deceive him into belief that he is going to become very spiritual. Yet, impressive religious activity, or even a position of importance in a church or fellowship, is not necessarily synonymous with true spirituality!

There is no doubt that seeking personal fulfilment in spiritual things can make a person vulnerable to deception. Whether you desire a great ministry for yourself, or wealth and riches, or a spouse, or a miraculous healing, or anything else—if you seek after that, some deceitful word or prophecy can very easily lead you astray. It is so easy to 'get a word' that confirms exactly what your heart is longing after! For example, a young woman wanting a husband can easily be led astray by a word of Scripture that seems to fit her situation exactly. It may not be the Lord speaking at all, but if she wants to believe it badly enough she may persuade herself that God has given her 'a word' and go headlong into something that in reality God had no part in!

We must not forget that Satan is able to quote texts to us, and will present us with such Scriptures as will appeal to our flesh or carnal mind in order to lead us astray. When he used this method to tempt Jesus, he was foiled because Jesus knew the other Scriptures too well to accept 'a word' simply because it fitted in with His circumstances! He would not accept a Scripture that merely justified fulfilling His own needs or accomplishing His own glory. That was no word from God even if it did come from the Bible! Jesus said, **'Begone Satan!'**

Recognising one's carnal ambitions and putting to death the works of the flesh are essential if one's own desires are not to lead one astray. Jeremiah had to warn even his most faithful scribe and disciple, Baruch, **'Do you seek great things for yourself? Seek them not'** (Jeremiah 45:5). Carnality is only dealt with by the cross. A 'cross-less' Christianity certainly appeals to the flesh, but Jesus said, **'anyone who does not carry his cross and follow me cannot be My disciple'** (Luke 14:27).

The Occult

Superstition, magic, ouija boards, astrology, fortune telling, spiritualism and mystic religions are all examples of occult practices. There are many more. They are ways into 'the fourth dimension'—the spiritual realm—but they all by-pass God. They are unconditionally forbidden by God, and are transgressions of the first commandment, **'You shall have no other gods before Me'**. Occult practice is idolatry.

Even though it may not be obvious at first sight, all false religions and cults have their roots in some kind of occult practice. In the occult one is dealing directly with evil, Satanic forces—often speaking and communing with the very powers of darkness that are in direct opposition to God and are under the authority of Satan. Through the occult, man seeks spiritual power and experience without the 'restriction' of obedience to God.

It is impossible for one who has even mildly 'dabbled' in any form of the occult not to incur some kind of spiritual bondage. It is in this area more than any other that the sins of one's forefathers can be a legacy of spiritual bondage even to the third and fourth generations. Abnormal fears, psychic tendencies, recurring depression, fanaticism, sexual perversions, uncontrollable temper, and many other serious spiritual ills can be the direct or indirect result of occult practice.

The Christian who, by bowing at one of Satan's modern-day shrines, has to a greater or lesser extent invited Satanic control into his life, appears to fall prey very easily to false beliefs following his (possibly shallow) conversion to Christ. The unknown, the mysterious and the inexplicable often have an irresistable appeal to him, and he may well indulge his curiosity and independence by delving into fringe doctrines which will lead him away from the all-important, fundamental truths of the faith.

If you are aware of any such link with occult powers of darkness, however insignificant it may seem, seek out a trusted servant of the Lord and openly confess all that needs to be brought to the light. Renounce those works of darkness, and ask him to pray in the name of Jesus for your deliverance from any lingering effects.

Peter had to exhort Simon the sorcerer to repent even after his conversion and baptism, as he was not free from the evil effects of occult bondage (Acts 8:21–23).

Ignorance and Misuse of the Scriptures

In countries where every man can own a Bible written in his own tongue, and may read it without fear of persecution, it seems a tragedy that so few believers bother to study the

Scriptures for themselves. The person who is ignorant of the Scriptures is ignorant of the most important document of all time—the one and only inspired volume of divine truth.

In many churches and fellowships there is a great emphasis placed on attending meetings. Worship, teaching and fellowship are deemed all-important. Christians seek 'the word of the Lord' through prophecies, messages and testimonies, through tapes or books, until there is neither time nor inclination to study the Scriptures. That has somehow become an optional extra!

There will always be certain preachers who do not handle the Scriptures honestly, but use them to back up their own doctrines or to justify their actions. This being so, are we willing to trust the interpretations of men to such an extent that we never go to the Bible ourselves to search out its real message?

Bible reading can often be a haphazard, 'hit-and-miss' affair. We open our Bibles at random and read a few verses hurriedly, hoping for something to inspire us for the day. Or we virtually replace our Bibles with devotional readings, or collections of Scripture verses for each day of the year. God is able to speak to us through these means too, but if we never read the Scripture in its context we may interpret random verses to mean something other than God intended, and be deceived. In fact, this kind of Scripture reading may differ little from looking for some auspicious word in the daily horoscopes!

Peter, who had heard God speak in an audible voice, declared, **'We have the prophetic word made more certain'** (2 Peter 1:19), showing that his confidence in the Scriptures had only increased by this experience. Consequently he encourages us all to pay attention to the sacred writings 'as to a lamp shining in a dark place', and to be wary of interpreting Scripture to suit our own opinions!

The Holy Spirit is the Author of the Book, and He reveals its truth to all who seek it with an honest and obedient heart.

The Bible is more than just a collection of promised blessings. It contains the whole counsel of God for man. The Scriptures are intended to do more than just bless or inspire us, more than simply confirm whether to take a new job or get married! So let us not neglect the proper use of this unique Book, but allow it to train us and equip us in the way that God intended.

Paul declared, **'All Scripture is inspired by God and profitable for teaching, for reproof, for correction, for training in righteousness, that the man of God may be complete, equipped for every good work'** (2 Timothy 3:16 RSV). This verse clearly explains the purpose of studying the Scriptures, and we would do well to check whether or not our own Bible reading is profiting and equipping us in all these ways! If it is, it will surely keep us from being deceived.

Neglect of Genuine Fellowship with God

Many Christians sadly neglect their devotional life. Some have turned from having a rather legalistic 'quiet time' each day to assuming that day-long fellowship with God requires no devotional time at all! We so often sink tiredly into bed at night with only a brief prayer, only to rise and rush into the day's activities in like manner. It is even possible to be very vocal in the prayer meeting, and yet be unable to manage more than a few sentences when alone with God!

There are differing levels of relationship in the world. An acquaintance is a person one knows and greets, and has tea with occasionally. A friend is someone with whom one spends more time, and develops a relationship of mutual liking and trust. But love and solemn vows bind a lasting relationship to a spouse. In what category would you place your relationship with God?

It is sin that separates man from God, and it is also sin that breaks a Christian's fellowship with Him (Isaiah 59:1–2). But whenever sins are forgiven, this relationship is restored and fellowship can be enjoyed once more. Jesus told us that it is the one who is forgiven much who loves Him much, so if our relationship with the Lord Jesus seems cold and unsatisfying, perhaps a fresh experience of His forgiveness would restore our first love. But if we do claim to love God, why is it so difficult to spend time alone with Him? Could it be that we love our meetings, our conferences, even our times of worship more than we love the Lord Himself?

The Christian life is, in essence, a walk with God. If the basic element of communion with Him is lacking, how will we learn to recognise His voice, or truly discern that which is of God from that which is of man or even Satan? The person who neglects to fellowship with God may be led unawares into fellowship with the counterfeit.

Disobedience to God

A person who appears to be confused, or to have strange ideas, may not be in as much need of sound teaching as of exhortation to be obedient to the Lord! A minister who is teaching false doctrine may be a person who refused to obey God over an issue in his personal life. If God speaks and we reply, 'No', why should He go on speaking and revealing further truth to us? Will He not wait until we respond on this matter before He takes us on to the next?

A young Christian may have in mind to marry, raise a family and settle comfortably into a successful business. But he begins to feel that God is calling him to lay aside his own plans and serve Him in mission. If he goes ahead with his own way, in spite of knowing God's calling, he is disobeying God. However, he may convince himself that he has chosen 'God's second best', that he had some kind of choice whether or not to obey God, and that all is still well. This man is already deceived.

Conversely, a young woman may desire a glamorous life of travel, the excitement of 'being a missionary', and completely ignore the leading of the Lord to look after an elderly or ailing parent at home. She goes her own way, convincing herself that she is serving God, but fails in her first responsibility. In reality she has deceived herself— further deception can easily follow.

Even when it appears to be difficult or unrewarding, God's will is always best. In the long run the path of disobedience will be the harder one. It is good to realise that God's will may not always coincide with our own will! Should a Christian knowingly disobey God, he may experience a difficult or 'dry' period until he repents and obeys. But if he wilfully continues in disobedience while maintaining all the outward forms of religion, he will soon go blindly down a wrong path without knowing it to be an error.

Obedience to God is not optional. We cannot choose to obey God in one matter and disobey Him in another. Peter stated categorically, **'We must obey God'** (Acts 5:29).

Absence of the Fear of the Lord

'The fear of the Lord is the beginning of wisdom' (Psalm 111:10).

Reverence and awe are attitudes that befit mortal man in his relationship with Almighty God. If, at any time, we become too familiar or over-confident in this relationship, our concept of God may be at fault and may require some adjustment.

There are some who are teaching today that man can 'command God'. They quote Isaiah 45:11, **'Command ye Me concerning the work of My hands'** (AV). This is taken to mean that a Christian has the authority to command God to act in certain situations rather than ask Him to do so in the more usual form of prayer. However, read in context, it seems far more likely that this verse is correctly translated as a question, **'Will you question Me about My children, or command Me concerning the work of My hands?'** (RSV, see also NIV & GNB).

Would the clay ask the potter why his vessel had no handles? Hardly! Far be it, then, for a mere man to question or command God! This whole passage is intended to make man realise who God is, and to inspire the proper awe and reverence He deserves. It is not fitting for man to consider telling the Almighty what to do!

The 'fearless' Christian perhaps imagines that God's love has somehow outweighed His righteousness, and so does not fear to disobey Him or to sin against a brother. He may exercise the gifts of the Spirit without caution or thought that there is any possibility of leading another astray. He may even go confidently into Christian ministry without seeking the dealings of God in his life, or without even a true commission or call.

The one who has no fear of God is described as a 'fool' in Scripture—he has not even begun to be wise. What man will be able to discern falsehood if he lacks even the beginning of wisdom? A healthy reverential fear of the Lord can turn a fool into a wise man. It can also turn a foolish Christian into a wise Christian—one who is not easily deceived.

Gullibility Concerning the Miraculous

Spiritualists are able to perform miracles of healing. Witchdoctors in heathen Africa speak in tongues. Witches are given words of knowledge (by evil spirits) and act upon them. Sects where ancestor worship is practised prophesy and see it come to pass. Fortune tellers can bring up something from your past that you had never told anyone. Mediums see visions, often of 'Jesus'. So-called 'faith healers' sometimes pray for people using the name of Jesus, though they may be professed atheists. Why then are we Christians so gullible as to believe that if we see a 'miracle' it must be of God?

Most of us have an undue regard for any minister able to show forth the miraculous, and will trust him implicitly. Some will trust a minister who has been 'baptised in the Spirit' to such a degree, that to suggest that discernment is still necessary seems like an insult! Yet Jesus did not say that we would recognise a prophet by his gifts or ministry, but by the fruit of his own life. Perhaps because of our humanity and its limitations, we earth-bound creatures are inevitably fascinated and impressed by the supernatural. From earliest childhood we have been in awe of the magician's wand! The good fairy and the wicked witch of childhood myths may have been put away, but the impression they made could still be with us, leaving us credulous, gullible and undiscerning when it comes to the miraculous in Christian ministry.

Many of us have experienced miraculous 'guidance'—a text of Scripture that gives us the go-ahead for a certain course of action. The Lord's people have often been directed supernaturally in ways like this. But even miraculous guidance need not always be of God. Some Christians have been led in the wrong direction by equally 'miraculous' words of Scripture or 'coincidences'. Some have been influenced to make major decisions that have ended in calamity. Does a miracle necessarily prove that you are in God's will? Satan is able to counterfeit such signs and miracles, and may well use these means in his attempt to lead us astray.

Yet in spite of this, God does perform miracles in our day —miracles that belong to a genuine work of the Holy Spirit, and which glorify the Lord Jesus Christ. In the realm of the miraculous, nothing is impossible with God. If there were no genuine miracles, there would be nothing to counterfeit!

It is also true that although Satan can counterfeit the miraculous, there are still many things he cannot do! Satan can never make a proud person truly humble, relieve a guilty conscience, conquer lust and greed, make an irritable, angry man gentle and patient, fully restore a broken marriage, or make a selfish person love others as himself! Wonders such as these, proved by time and testing, can only be performed by the Lord Jesus Christ.

Genuine miracles go together with the proclamation of God's word. **'And they went out and preached everywhere, while the Lord worked with them, and confirmed the word by the signs that followed'** (Mark 16:20). The preaching of the true word of God will bring forth genuine miracles. May God grant us discernment between the genuine and the counterfeit!

*　*　*　*　*

As you have read this chapter, perhaps God has shown you areas of your life where you are vulnerable to deception, or where to a greater or lesser extent you have been deceived. Do not be discouraged! *God has a purpose in allowing false prophets!*

Moses added this illuminating statement to his teaching about false prophets, *'The Lord your God is testing you to find out whether you love him with all your heart and with all your soul'* (Deuteronomy 13:3 NIV).

God is still in control. Jesus Christ is head of His church and He knows what is going on there. He tests His children to see if they love Him above all else! If perhaps you have failed one such test, and if false prophets or teachers have deceived you and led you astray by one means or another, take heart—there are always new beginnings with God. Return to the Lord confessing your faults, and *ask Him to show you the remedy that applies to you.* Then start afresh with renewed faith. The understanding gained in one such experience will be turned into strength for future contests, and your deepening knowledge of His grace will richly increase your love for Him.

8
The End

**'On that day many will say to me,
"Lord, Lord, did we not prophesy in your name,
and cast our demons in your name,
and do many mighty works in your name?"
And then I will declare to them**

"I NEVER KNEW YOU

depart from me, you evildoers"'

This conversation between the Lord Jesus and those who claim to have ministered in His name will take place on the Day of Judgment. As we look at this disquieting passage of Scripture, three vital questions confront us which we must answer before bringing this subject to its conclusion.

Will I Recognise a False Prophet?

Living, as we do, before the ultimate exposure of that coming Day, are we confident that we will be able to recognise a false prophet? Will we in fact spot the 'wolf' among the sheep? We may well wonder, in the face of the deceptive 'sheep's clothing' along with impressive miraculous works and subtly appealing teachings, if we will not be among those who are lured away from the truth and deceived.

The Lord Jesus will deal in all finality with false prophets on the Day of Judgment, but does this mean that we can ignore the matter now? No, the problem of false prophets needs to be handled correctly in the church today. How then should we tackle such a problem if it arises in our midst?

In order to discern whether a prophet is truly of God or not, we know that above all else *we must look at the fruit being manifested in his life.* Is the fruit of the Spirit clearly growing in increasing measure in that prophet's life, or do we notice with alarm that the works of the flesh are much more in evidence? Concerning his ministry, what is the main thrust of his message? Is it in line with the gospel as revealed in Scripture or does it veer away in one direction or another? Are there lasting results that bring glory to God, or has his ministry left confusion, division and a trail of tragedies in its wake? Perhaps the fact that false apostles had ministered undiscerned in the Corinthian church was one of the main reasons for the multitude of troubles Paul found there—even in spite of Peter's, Apollos's and his own powerful ministries!

Suppose you become aware that you have been deceived through a false ministry, what are you going to do about it? The right course of action is not always immediately obvious, so in the first place—and since every case is different—we must make room for the leading of the Holy Spirit. It is important that we do not become legalistic in our attitude, or put ourselves in the place of God who alone may act as Judge. Nevertheless, the Holy Spirit will not contradict the principles laid down in Scripture, or go against that which God has revealed there about this important subject. Rather, as we seek God and look in His word for instruction, the Holy Spirit will show us how to handle each issue as it comes up.

Before doing anything else, a Christian who believes that he has been deceived must first examine his own life before God. It will not help simply to see what is wrong in the minister or the leader of your fellowship, if you are not willing to see first the faults in your own heart that led you in that direction! Only if you will honestly evaluate your own spiritual condition before God, and be willing to put right all that may have been out of order there, will you be on right ground to go any further.

But going on from here, what do the Scriptures actually teach? Do they give us any specific instruction that might help us to know what to do?

It was because Paul felt responsible for the spiritual welfare of the body of believers wherever he went, that he repeatedly warned them against those who were false within the church. **'Have nothing to do with them'** (2 Timothy 3:5), **'Keep away from them'** (Romans 16:17), he said. He told Titus; **'Reject a factious man after a first and a second warning'** (Titus 3:10). At times he even named those in question, as when he warned Timothy to be on his guard against Alexander who had 'vigorously opposed' his teaching (Timothy 4:15), and when he disciplined Hymenaeus and Alexander by putting them out of the church (1 Timothy 1:20). These men were all causing trouble of one kind or another, and may well have been false prophets.

The apostle John also specifically warned the believers against Diotrephes, who was probably a leading elder in one of the churches he wrote to. This man loved 'to be first among them', was intensely critical and rejected the apostle's teaching. Note what John said, **'If I come, I will call attention to his *deeds*'** (3 John 9–10). Of another whose teachings were contradictory to the teachings of Christ, he warned, **'Do not receive him into your house, and do not give him a greeting'** (2 John 10).

The apostles were not weak where something was wrong. Paul acted on the same principle as when he dealt with sin. First he warned the offender to repent, then he gave a second warning in case he had not fully understood. But if he stubbornly persisted in his error, *then Paul warned others against him.* The apostle even **'delivered to Satan'** those who continued in evil ways, putting them out of the church altogether (1 Timothy 1:20, 1 Corinthians 5:5). Sin must be purged from the church, and if the person clings to his sin, then that person must go. If he will not go, then let the believers separate from him, and leave him. Sin is contagious, it will spread. Treat it like cancer, or gangrene! God is not tolerant of sin and neither should we be.

Cancer that is not removed in its early stages can soon become inoperable—it will spread to other parts of the body and result in eventual death. Failure to deal with a false prophet could have equally devastating spiritual consequences. How much better to lose a cancerous member of the body, than that the whole body die!

Consequently if false prophets refuse to repent when they are warned, they should be asked to leave the church. But if unrepentant false prophets are the ones in authority, then we must be prepared to leave them. Responsible pastors and shepherds will also warn others, even as Paul and John did.

Will a False Prophet Recognise Himself?

It is always possible that a minister will recognise that not only has he himself been deceived, but that he has also been deceiving others and leading them astray. God is faithful both to warn a false prophet and to show him the way back to the right path. Yet in reality it is very difficult for a minister to admit that he has been wrong, and more difficult still to humble himself to make the necessary apologies or restitution. Only a deep work of grace can accomplish this. However, with God nothing is impossible, and we must never judge a person to be beyond the grace of God. God alone may judge thus.

If we realise that a false prophet is often a successful person with a following, one who is able to preach impressive sermons and exercise miraculous gifts, then we can more easily understand his surprise when the Lord Jesus does not acknowledge him on Judgment Day. After all, he has probably spent most of his life, as he thought, ministering in the name of Jesus, and he has proof of success in the many impressive works that have accompanied his ministry! When he presents his credentials to the Lord, confident of all that he has accomplished in His name, he expects to be rewarded and given his crown! Alas, even in the presence of the Judge on His throne, he does not recognise himself as false!

If a prophet continues in evil ways in spite of being convicted by his own conscience, warned by colleagues and given opportunities to repent by God Himself, then he has deliberately and knowingly chosen that path. His conscience has become seared as with a hot iron, his pride has deceived him into thinking himself above correction, and on the very Day of Judgment he has the audacity to argue with the Lord and Judge of all!

The evidence strongly suggests that false prophets neither recognise themselves as such here, nor on the very day they stand before God. One can only surmise that their repeated rejection of warnings and opportunities to repent strengthens them in their delusion and falsehood, until God Himself gives them over to reap their due reward.

'They perish because they refused to love the truth and so be saved. For this reason God sends them a powerful delusion so that they will believe

**the lie, and so that all will be condemned who have
not believed the truth but have delighted in
wickedness'** (2 Thessalonians 2:10–12 NIV).

Will the Lord Jesus Recognise a False Prophet?

Finally then, from the text quoted at the head of the
chapter, we see how the Lord Jesus regards the false
prophet. He declares that He has never known him! Clearly
no real relationship between this man and the Lord ever
existed, so He makes it plain that He does not recognise
him as His own. But He does, however, recognise him for
what he is—He recognises that he is an 'evildoer'! One
thing is certain, no-one can pull the wool over the eyes of
the Lord. He will not be deceived! **'All things are open
and laid bare to the eyes of Him with whom we have
to do'** (Hebrews 4:13).

On the Day of Judgment, the criteria will not be the
number of prophecies you have given, or the demons you
have cast out, or the wonderful works you claim to have
done in His name, but *whether or not Jesus recognises you as
His, and whether or not you have turned from evil.*

The question of evil in our world is very complex, and
has vexed the minds of scholars and theologians over the
centuries. How is it that a person desiring to preach from
the Bible, often wanting to help others and to 'serve God',
should become the one who most warrants His wrath and
judgment? Should not God congratulate the person who has
spent his life endeavouring to serve Him in the way he
thought best?

Satan was in the position of 'anointed cherub', a heavenly
being of great power and authority under God. If I may put
it this way, he had received a great God-given ministry. But
without being tempted or deceived, in the full light of his
knowledge of God, he desired to set himself up as the

Highest Authority. He rebelled against God by deliberate choice.

Those in positions of spiritual authority in the church as ministers, prophets, shepherds, pastors or leaders, have the greatest temptation of all—'to be as God'. Yet a minister is a servant of God. His authority comes from his submission to The Authority. The prophet who desires the authority of God while rejecting obedience to God, is in fact following the way of Satan—rebellion!

Yet in spite of all this, even Satan has a place in God's plan. God's children must learn to hate and reject all evil— how could they do this if there were none? In a similar way, God uses false prophets to test and sift His children, and to produce in them those qualities He desires. Yet the cry of all those who have been hurt and wounded, and of those who are being opposed or slandered, may well echo that of the martyrs, **'How long, O Lord?'** (Revelation 6:10). We can, however, rely upon God's justice. He will expose and deal with evil. Let us take comfort from these reassuring words of Scripture, **'Righteousness and justice are the foundation of Thy throne'** (Psalms 89:14) and, **'The triumphing of the wicked is short'** (Job 20:5).

The strongest words of judgment in the whole Bible are written not of murderers, witches or prostitutes, but of so-called 'teachers' and 'shepherds' who have deceived and exploited God's flock. **'Their condemnation has long been hanging over them'**, writes Peter (2 Peter 2:3 NIV) and Jude declares, **'For them the black darkness has been reserved for ever'** (Jude 13).

For the false prophet, then, this is the end. The end of his success, the end of his power, the end of his pleasures, the end of his exploitation of others, the end of his glory.

Eternity, however, has no end. Eternal joy and reward and a share in the glorious reign of Christ Himself awaits every true believer. But the one who follows a deceiver and shares in his ways, rejecting opportunities to repent and turn back to the truth, he will also share his eternal loss.

Let us make sure that we do not follow false prophets to their appointed destiny!

Epilogue

**Everyone who lives on milk
lacks experience in the word of righteousness
since he is an infant
But solid food is for the mature
whose faculties have been exercised and**

TRAINED TO DISCERN

between good and evil

The thread that weaves its way through every chapter of this book is the theme of discernment. Without the ability to discern, all that we have read so far will remain mere head-knowledge, and we will be unable to put it to use in our daily lives. So, what is discernment, and how do we acquire it?

Discernment is the ability to distinguish between good and evil. From the very beginning Satan put a cloak over evil in order to hide its true nature—he managed to make evil appear 'good'. In the Garden of Eden, Eve fell to Satan's deception, not discerning that what she was choosing was evil. She believed that the fruit of the forbidden tree was 'good'. Adam also fell—he disobeyed the command of God and plunged the whole human race into disobedience.

Subsequently man has become so confused as to what is

good and what is evil that all too often his conscience is brushed aside as it points out that he has chosen evil while thinking it to be good. Many think it 'good' to spend their lives acquiring wealth and possessions, or to enjoy as many pleasures as possible. Others will justify the use of lies and deceit, thinking it 'good' if it will help to further their cause. Churchmen of the past found it 'good' to burn godly men and women at the stake, calling them heretics. Hitler was even convinced that it was 'good' to exterminate the whole Jewish race! It is in fact possible to find a 'good' reason for almost anything man wants to do. But what is 'good'? Is it whatever benefits people? Is it the thing that is most expedient?

Similarly we could ask, 'What is evil?' But in fact, rather than attempt to make definitions and draw lines of demarcation, or have someone decide for us 'this is good' and 'that is evil', *our real need is for each one of us to exercise his own ability to discern.*

There are many things that have the appearance of being good, but when the cloak is lifted off they are found to be evil. It may seem good that the minister makes an appeal for finances 'for the Lord's work', but if there is deceit and misuse of funds behind that appeal, it is not good, it is evil. Perhaps a married woman thinks it is good to attend Bible studies and prayer meetings during the week, but if she is neglecting her husband and family by doing so, it is not good, it is evil. The minister may preach a 'good' message from the Bible, but if it subtly undermines the truths set forth elsewhere in the same Bible, it is not good, it is evil.

Deception is Satan's chief tactic. He began to wield this tool in the Garden of Eden, and he will continue to trick and deceive men into choosing evil until his efforts culminate in the Antichrist. Without the ability to discern, to see through the cover that he puts over evil in order to

117

make it appear 'good', every one of us will fall prey to deception in one form or another.

Then how can we be 'trained to discern', as our text puts it? First of all, discernment is an attribute of a mature person. An infant will as happily put a lump of coal in his mouth as a potato! Not so the adult, who has learned what is good for him as he has grown in understanding and experience. So if we are to develop the ability to discern in spiritual things, *it is essential that we grow toward spiritual maturity.*

For growth to begin, we know that an 'infant' Christian needs to be nourished with **'the pure milk of the word'** (1 Peter 2:2). However, in order to reach maturity, his diet of 'milk' must gradually be replaced with **'solid food'** (Hebrews 5:13). The books, sermons, and Bible studies prepared by others will no longer be enough. The growing Christian needs to be able to 'feed himself' from the Scriptures, and so acquire the ability to distinguish between the different kinds of 'food' presented to him by others. 'Solid food' needs to be 'chewed over', and the word of righteousness can sometimes be 'difficult to swallow'!

'The word of God is . . . sharper than any two-edged sword, piercing to the division of soul and spirit, . . . *and discerning the thoughts and intentions of the heart'* (Hebrews 4:12 RSV). The person whose mind is being renewed and transformed by the word of God will be increasingly equipped to distinguish between good and evil, even when evil is cloaked with apparent good, or when man's own soul counterfeits the working of God. He will also be able to perceive the motives which lie behind many seemingly 'good' words and deeds.

But the 'sermon-tasting Christian', or the 'meeting addict', or the one who unquestioningly accepts everything he hears or reads, or the person who picks out what he likes to hear and discards all else, will remain in spiritual infancy. He will not mature. Neither will he learn to discern.

In addition to this, being 'trained to discern' also involves *understanding Satan's tactics in our own lives*. A young Christian initially recognises and puts away the more obvious 'evils' from his life when he is converted, but the process must not end there. We need to become more aware of Satan's tactics and more alert as time progresses. A lifetime may be too short to unravel some of the subtleties of Satan's deception and to purge out the forms of 'evil' which mar and spoil the lives of supposedly mature Christians. If we gloss over such things as impure motives, deceitfulness and pretence, resentment, touchiness, criticism and self-righteousness, hurtful remarks, grumbling and complaining, or even laziness, self-indulgence and thoughtlessness in ourselves, we will by-pass our best training ground for discernment!

As we increasingly discern what is 'evil' and deal with it in our own lives, we will be exercising our faculties and training ourselves to discern between good and evil in every other situation.

Judging ourselves is not only essential in being 'trained to discern', it can also save us from becoming critical and passing judgment on others. Not every person who makes a mistake, or errs in some point of doctrine, or falls in one way or another is a false prophet! Our own continuing experience of God's grace will enable us to love and help those who are stumbling, and also to forgive and pray for any who have harmed or misled us. In the love of God even the deepest wounds can heal and bitterness can melt away. By heeding the instruction of the Lord we can come through our most difficult experiences enriched and wiser, and knowing Him better than we did before.

God reigns over all in His sovereign power and authority.

He was and is and always will be in control of all that happens. As we begin to experience the ways in which God makes all things work together for our ultimate good, our trust in Him will increase and grow strong. God is able to keep us from falling prey to false prophets, and will do so as long as we walk in fellowship with Him, acknowledging Him as Lord in every area of our lives. Our growth in maturity and discernment will not only safeguard us from being deceived and unknowingly choosing evil, but it will also be accompanied by an increasing knowledge, love and deep adoration of our Lord Jesus Christ. As a result, our hearts will bow before Him in thankfulness and in true worship at His infinite greatness!

**'Now to Him who is able to keep you from falling
and to present you without blemish
before the presence of His glory with rejoicing,
to the only God, our Saviour
through Jesus Christ our Lord,
be glory, majesty, dominion, and authority,
before all time and now and for ever.**

AMEN'.   (Jude 24–25 RSV)

Scripture References

The main sources of reference used in this book are listed below in their contexts. This is not intended to be an exhaustive list of Scripture references for any of the subjects mentioned, but it is given here for any reader who might wish to examine the Biblical basis for this study.

Old Testament

Moses

Deuteronomy 13:1–5	False prophets
18:20–22	False prophets

Jeremiah

Jeremiah 1:4–10	The prophet's call
7:1–11	Unacceptable worship
14:14	False prophets
23:1–2, 9–40	False prophets
29:8–9	False prophets
Lamentations 2:14	False prophets

Ezekiel

Ezekiel 13:1–23	False prophets
34:1–10	False shepherds

Amos

Amos 5:21–24	Unacceptable worship

Micah

Micah 3:5–12	False prophets

New Testament

Jesus

Matthew 7:15–23	False prophets
24:1–24	False prophets and false Christs
Mark 13:1–23	False prophets and false Christs
John 10:1–16	The Good Shepherd and the hireling

Paul

2 Corinthians 11:4, 13–15	False apostles
Galatians 1:6–9	False teachers and a false gospel
2 Thessalonians 2:3–12	The Antichrist
1 Timothy 1:3–7, 4:1–3, 6:3–10	False teachers
2 Timothy 2:17–18	False teachers
3:1–9, 4:3–4	False believers and teachers
1 Timothy 1:3–5, 18–19	Ministerial requirements
3:1–13, 4:6–16	Ministerial requirements
5:17–22, 6:11–21	Ministerial requirements
2 Timothy 2, 3:14–4:5	Ministerial requirements
Titus 1:5–9, 2:1–15, 3:1–14	Ministerial requirements

Peter

2 Peter 2:1–22	False teachers

Jude

Jude 3–19	False teachers

John

1 John 2:18–23, 26	Antichrists
4:1–3	False prophets
2 John 7	Deceivers
3 John 9–10	A false elder
Revelation 13:11–18, 16:13–14, 19:20, 20:10	The False Prophet

Scripture References for Chapter Headings

Chapter		
1.		Mark 13:22
2.		Matthew 7:15 (RSV)
3.	(1)	Titus 1:7 (NIV)
	(2)	Matthew 7:15 (RSV)
4.		2 Corinthians 11:4, 13 (RSV)
5.	(1)	1 Timothy 1:5
	(2)	Matthew 24:11 (RSV)
6.	(1)	Revelation 13:11–18, 19:20
	(2)	1 John 4:1 (RSV)
7.		2 Corinthians 13:5
8.		Matthew 7:22–23 (RSV)
Epilogue		Hebrews 5:13–14